AF261451

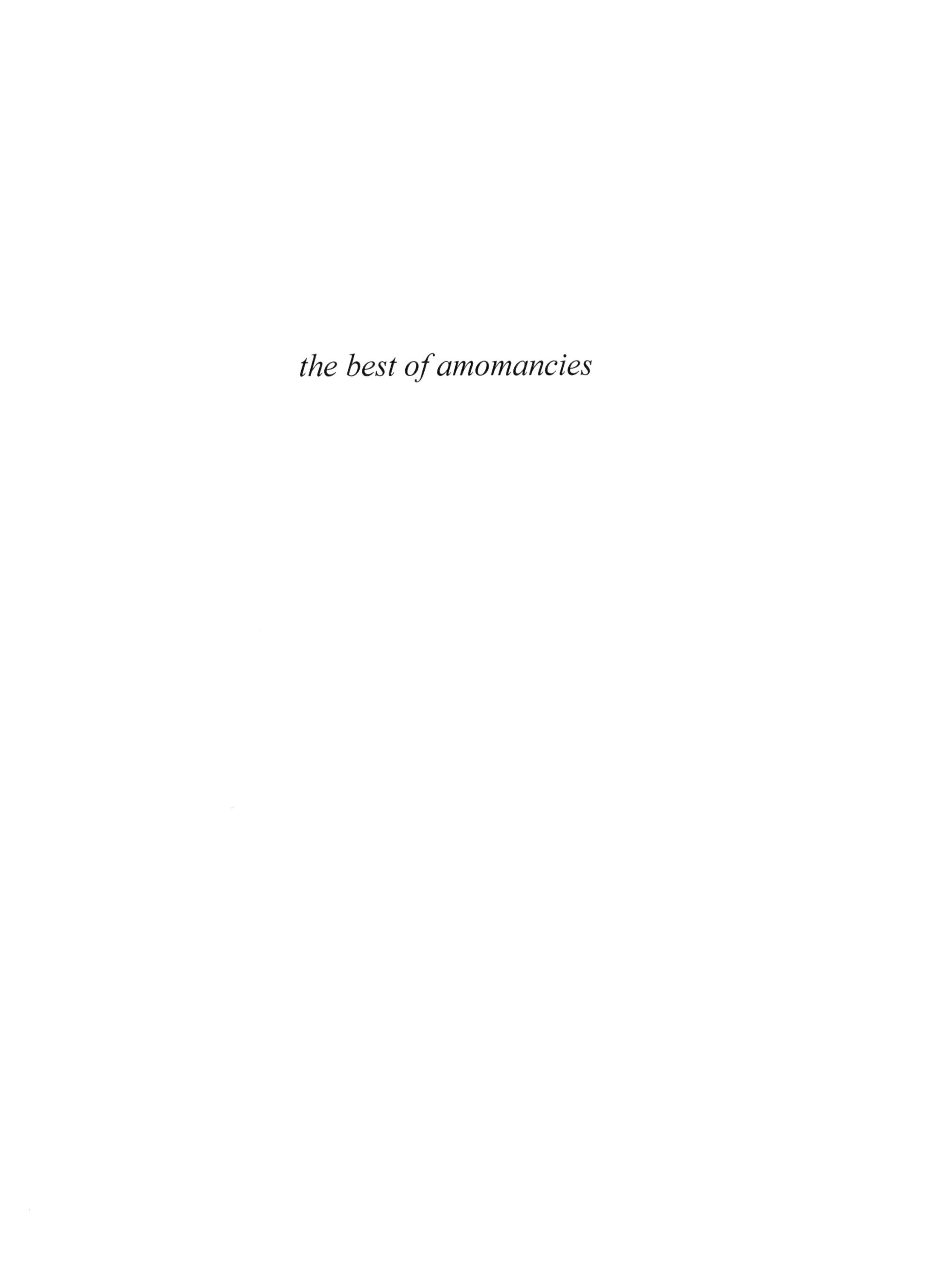

the best of amomancies

the best of amomancies

By way of Introduction

In the beginning was the word. And the word was **amote**. I've always been a fan of words and how they are created and evolve. So one day I noticed (I am sure someone else had to have noticed before me) that "amo te", literally "I love you" in Latin, when you dropped the space, became a single word that could mean "to speak of love", just as to speak in favor of something is to promote or to speak out is to emote.

Soon after I used it in a few poems. The notion of labelling love poems or love letters as "amotation" occurred to me. Soon thereafter this was followed by a reader labelling me an "amomancer", one who weaves spells with words of love, which suggested that such love spells, taking the form of letters or poems were, you guessed it, "**amomancies**".

Now let's come at it a different way. A few years ago, working with models I knew to illustrate my poems for various online sites, I hit upon the idea for a magazine that would go all out into that standard.

Originally conceived as "Red", then later "EJT" (the initials of Percy Bysshe Shelley's brave friend Edward James Trelawny), I finally set upon the name "amomancies", then started the arduous work of selling the notion to photographers and models. For the original issue I decided to build it as a proof of concept, in case it cratered, only using my own poetry…I found approval for the idea with the models and photographers.

The first issue, with my constant collaborator Mariya Andriichuk on the cover, premiered in August of 2014. It was downloadable as a pdf or could be ordered in print version. I had hoped for a few hundred readers. The first issue had thousands. Concept proven.

Realizing the amount of work required to put together each issue, I set it as a quarterly magazine and got to work recruiting more models and photographers, and more poets. I set the "rule of seven" where a poet or model would not, except under exceptional circumstances, appear more than seven times in a given issue (you'll notice echoes of that rule here, with no poet appearing more than seven times in this book, and only two of the models appearing more than that).

The rigors of putting out the magazine became debilitating, so I went on hiatus a few times over the next three years (we are currently on an extended hiatus, I have no doubt but that amomancies shall return.) And eventually the notion occurred, with the founding of Venetian Spider Press, to put out a "best of amomancies" volume. Which meant pursuing all of the poets and photographers and models who had previously appeared in the magazine. Only two or three of the models declined. Only one poet did. Several of the models I had trouble reaching, despite assorted attempts to make contact. That was difficult for me, as some of the ones we could not get in touch with, at least by deadline time, represented some pretty fantastic images.

Then we had to sort through and keep this volume to a reasonable thickness…

…and here it is. I want to thank and acknowledge, not only the contributors, but the editorial staff of amomancies, including Daniel McTaggart, Mariya Andriichuk, Peri DeVault, Ashley O'Neill, and Elric DeVault. You guys rock.

Respectfully

William F. DeVault
Amomancer, founder and editor-in-chief, amomancies magazine

the best of amomancies

the best of amomancies

Table of Contents (in order of manifestation)

Blessed by Fire
Poem: Edilson Afonso Ferreira   Image: Paulina Mieczkowska
The Sacred Heart of Persephone
Poem: Amberly mason   Image: Mariya Andriichuk
Her Finger Does the Smoothest Talking
Poem: Adrian Ernesto Cepeda   Image: Aysha J. Nasser
Midnight Muse in a Convenience Store
Poem: Daniel McTaggart   Image: Paulina Mieczkowska
Two People
Poem: Debbie Tosun Kilday   Image: Goce Alice
Soundtrack
Poem: Lynn White   Image: Ifigenia Tsitsa
Dinner at Golden Corral Buffet
Poem: Jackie Chou   Image: Goce Alice
Mess of Thrown Off Clothes
Poem: Strider Marcus Jones   Image: Paulina Mieczkowska
Four-legged Meadow Lark
Poem: Catherine Katey Johnson   Image: Mariya Andriichuk
Romance Litters the Floor
Poem: Amberly Mason   Image: Goce Alice
A Woman Does Not Have to Wait
Poem: Strider Marcus Jones   Image: Ifigenia Tsitsa
Grave Lover:
Poem: Robert Wilson   Image: Aysha J. Nasser
Meeting
Poem: Lynn White   Image: Inga Medvedev
He Plays His Flamenco Guitar
Poem: Strider Marcus Jones   Image: Marion Volant
pretty pretty soul
Poem: William F. DeVault   Image: Mariya Andriichuk
Two Poems
Poem: Nivedita Dey   Image: Goce Alice
Bowie Me
Poem: Daniel de Culla   Image: Aysha J. Nasser
Alpha and Omega
Poem: Amberly Mason   Image: Ifigenia Tsitsa
The Cries of the Succubi
Poem: Amelia Vandergast   Image: Inga Medvedev
Aphrodite's Risk
Poem: Daniel McTaggart   Image: Mariya Andriichuk
Dinner Date
Poem: Shloka Shankar   Image: Goce Alice
Unzipping Her Pleasure of Psalms 113:105
Poem: Adrian Ernesto Cepeda   Image: Jessica Lorraine Zickefoose
The Lioness
Poem: Chris Riddell   Image: Goce Alice

the best of amomancies

An American Night
Poem: Daniel McTaggart   Image: Mariya Andriichuk
Midnight and Mornings
Poem: Strider Marcus Jones   Image: Inga Medvedev
Spirit Horse
Poem: Theodore Webb   Image: Aysha J. Nasser
The Madrigal of Voices
Poem: Strider Marcus Jones   Image: Paulina Mieczkowska
It Wouldn't Be Make Believe if You Believed in Me
Poem: Marianne Peel   Image: Mariya Andriichuk
Late Night Phone Call
Poem: Nate Maxson   Image: Aysha Nasser
Butterfly Effect
Poem: Clinton Van Inman   Image: Jessica Lorraine Zickefoose
The Phoenix Rises in Venus
Poem: Amberly Mason   Image: Goce Alice
Eye Back to Basics
Poem: One Single Rose   Image: Paulina Mieczkowska
Feels Like 40c
Poem: R.A. Lucas   Image: Marion Volant
Blue
Poem: Lynn White   Image: Aysha J. Nasser
cithara song, strummed lightly as the sun leaps the horizon
Poem: William F. DeVault   Image: Marlita Polner
The Fabric of Creation
Poem: Mike Essiq   Image: Mariya Andriichuk
Sweet Smoke
Poem: Daniel McTaggart   Image: Aysha J. Nasser
Interstices
Poem: Chris Riddell   Image: Mariya Andriichuk
Beckoning
Poem: Jessica Lorraine Zickefoose   Image: Hannah Young
Wet Affection
Poem: Don Kingfisher Campbell   Image: Jessica Lorraine Zickefoose
The Existentialism of a Guaranteed Tomorrow
Poem: Robert Wilson   Image: Ifigenia Tsitsa
Love Is, All Is
Poem: Strider Marcus Jones   Image: Mariya Andriichuk
Damsel of Delights
Poem: Mike Essiq   Image: Mariya Andriichuk
horoscope: leo/virgo
Poem: Anu Mahadev   Image: Paulina Mieczkowska
Advantage
Poem: Catherine Katey Johnson   Image: Ifigenia Tsitsa
Off the road
Poem: Ed Jay   Image: Paulina Mieczkowska
Abandon
Poem: Kathy Anderson   Image: Ifigenia Tsitsa

the best of amomancies

Myth or Legend
Poem: Larry Jaffe

Image: Mariya Andriichuk

Eye Contact
Poem: Lynn White

Image: Paulina Mieczkowska

Getting Married
Poem: Lynn White

Image: Ifigenia Tsitsa

Convenience Store Coquette
Poem: Daniel McTaggart

Image: Mariya Andriichuk

Lover's Desire
Poem: Amitabh Vikram

Image: Jessica Lorraine Zickefoose

Vodka and Condoms
Poem: William F. DeVault

Image: Paulina Mieczkowska

Desire
Poem: Hardeep Sabharwal

Image: Paulina Mieczkowska

Last Poem for H.
Poem: Nate Maxson

Image: Mariya Andriichuk

First Love
Poem: Saddiq Dzukogi

Image: Jessica Lorraine Zickefoose

November Sky
Poem: Jessica Lorraine Zickefoose

Image: Paulina Mieczkowska

soubrette
Poem: William F. DeVault

Image: Jessica Lorraine Zickefoose

Dilemma
Poem: Amitabh Vikram

Image: Mariya Andriichuk

Picking Up Chicks at the Psych Ward
Poem: Robert Wilson

Image: Mariya Andriichuk

Fireflies
Poem: Clinton Van Inman

Image: Paulina Mieczkowska

I'm Sorry We Were Ever Young
Poem: Robert Wilson

Image: Paulina Mieczkowska

swerve (flirt)
Poem: William F. DeVault

Image: Mariya Andriichuk

dance naked in the sky
Poem: William F. DeVault

Image: Paulina Mieczkowska

Anticipation
Poem: Marianne Peel

Image: Mariya Andriichuk

Dream Lovers
Poem: Lynn White

Image: Paulina Mieczkowska

Electric Tang
Poem: Daniel McTaggart

Image: Mariya Andriichuk

Narcissus
Poem: Mathias Jansson

Image: Paulina Mieczkowska

I Know My Way to Sinking
Poem: Kushal Poddar

Image: Marion Volant

the best of amomancies

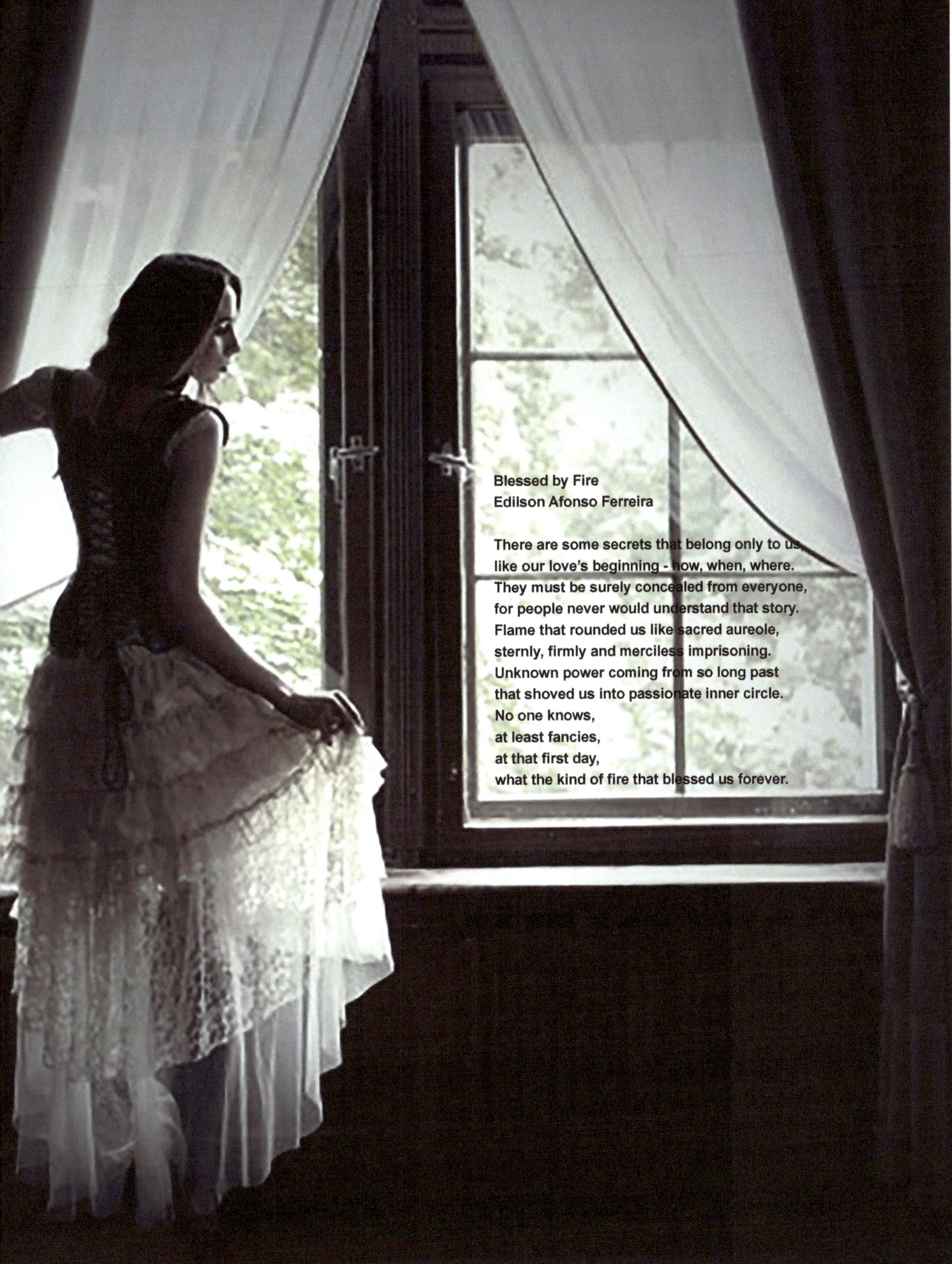

Blessed by Fire
Edilson Afonso Ferreira

There are some secrets that belong only to us,
like our love's beginning - how, when, where.
They must be surely concealed from everyone,
for people never would understand that story.
Flame that rounded us like sacred aureole,
sternly, firmly and merciless imprisoning.
Unknown power coming from so long past
that shoved us into passionate inner circle.
No one knows,
at least fancies,
at that first day,
what the kind of fire that blessed us forever.

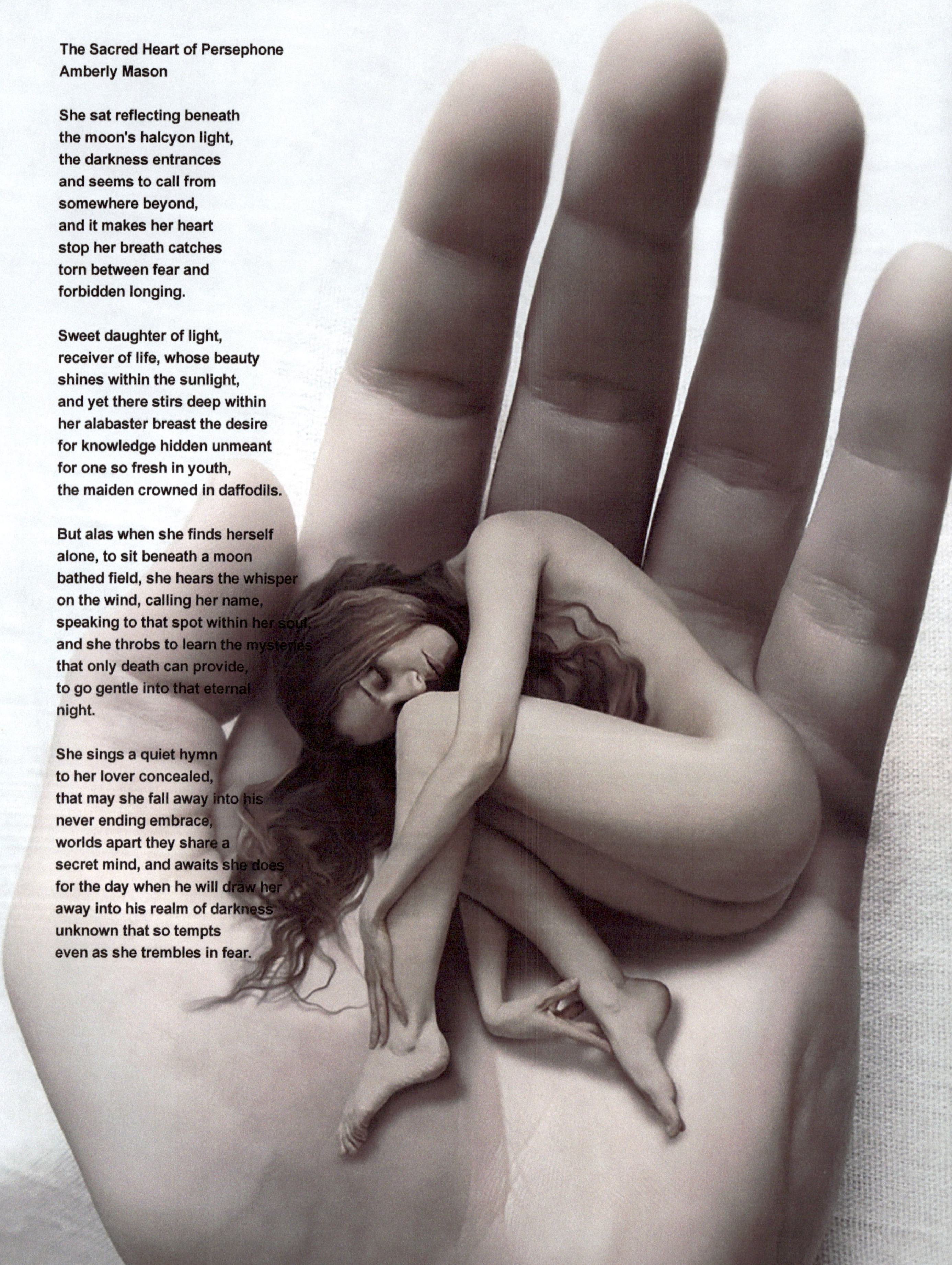

The Sacred Heart of Persephone
Amberly Mason

She sat reflecting beneath
the moon's halcyon light,
the darkness entrances
and seems to call from
somewhere beyond,
and it makes her heart
stop her breath catches
torn between fear and
forbidden longing.

Sweet daughter of light,
receiver of life, whose beauty
shines within the sunlight,
and yet there stirs deep within
her alabaster breast the desire
for knowledge hidden unmeant
for one so fresh in youth,
the maiden crowned in daffodils.

But alas when she finds herself
alone, to sit beneath a moon
bathed field, she hears the whisper
on the wind, calling her name,
speaking to that spot within her soul,
and she throbs to learn the mysteries
that only death can provide,
to go gentle into that eternal
night.

She sings a quiet hymn
to her lover concealed,
that may she fall away into his
never ending embrace,
worlds apart they share a
secret mind, and awaits she does
for the day when he will draw her
away into his realm of darkness
unknown that so tempts
even as she trembles in fear.

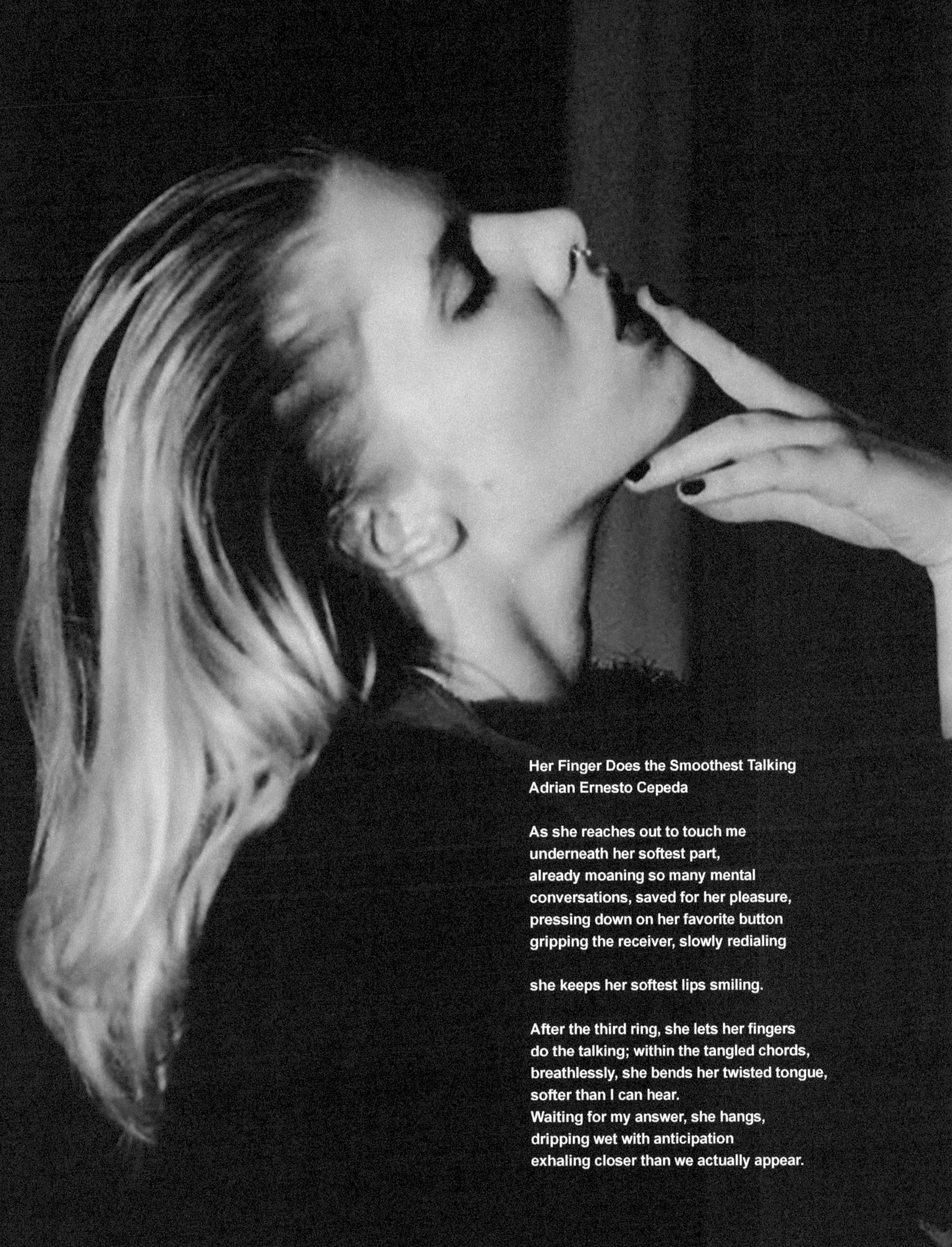

Her Finger Does the Smoothest Talking
Adrian Ernesto Cepeda

As she reaches out to touch me
underneath her softest part,
already moaning so many mental
conversations, saved for her pleasure,
pressing down on her favorite button
gripping the receiver, slowly redialing

she keeps her softest lips smiling.

After the third ring, she lets her fingers
do the talking; within the tangled chords,
breathlessly, she bends her twisted tongue,
softer than I can hear.
Waiting for my answer, she hangs,
dripping wet with anticipation
exhaling closer than we actually appear.

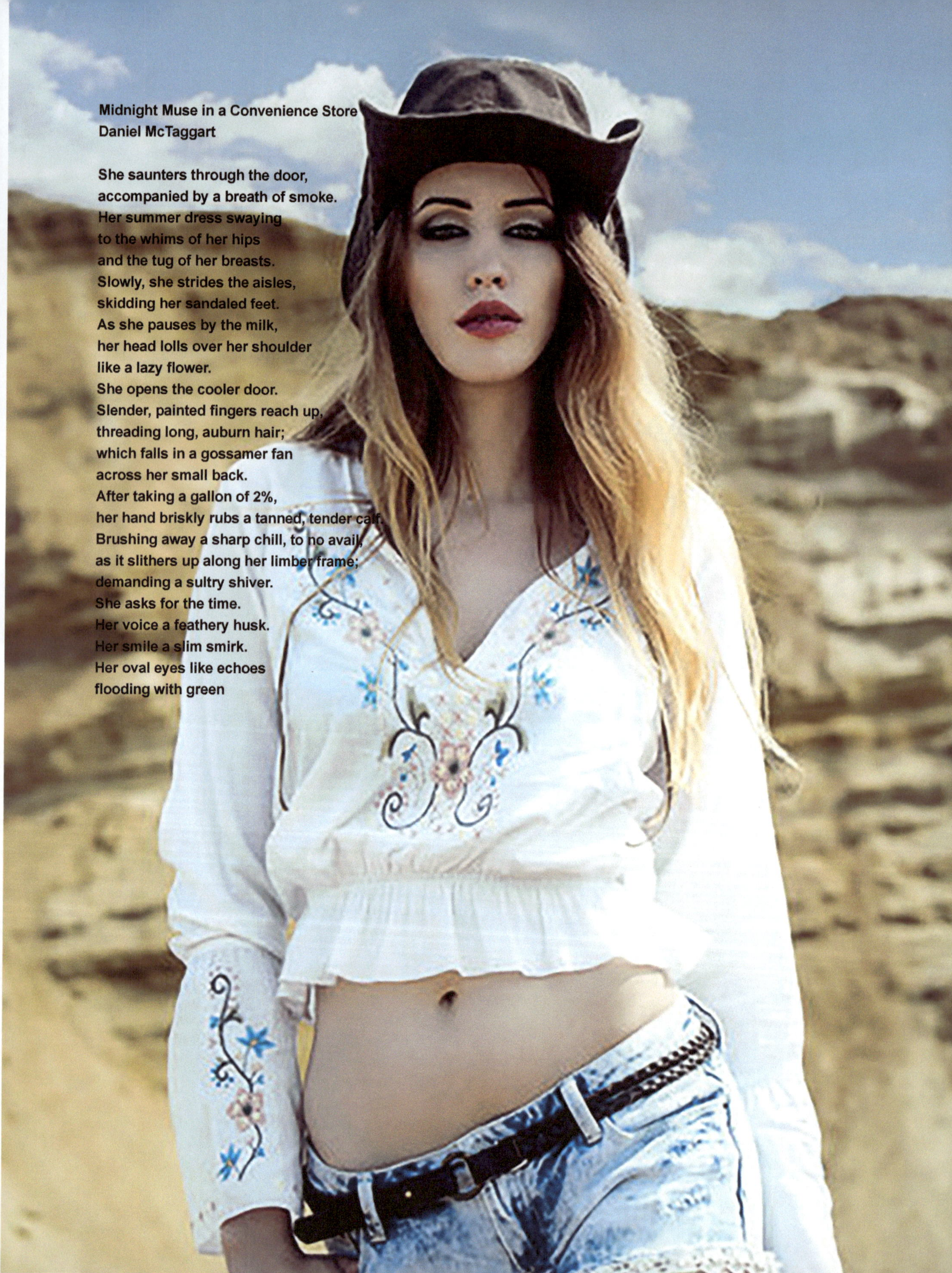

Midnight Muse in a Convenience Store
Daniel McTaggart

She saunters through the door,
accompanied by a breath of smoke.
Her summer dress swaying
to the whims of her hips
and the tug of her breasts.
Slowly, she strides the aisles,
skidding her sandaled feet.
As she pauses by the milk,
her head lolls over her shoulder
like a lazy flower.
She opens the cooler door.
Slender, painted fingers reach up,
threading long, auburn hair;
which falls in a gossamer fan
across her small back.
After taking a gallon of 2%,
her hand briskly rubs a tanned, tender calf.
Brushing away a sharp chill, to no avail,
as it slithers up along her limber frame;
demanding a sultry shiver.
She asks for the time.
Her voice a feathery husk.
Her smile a slim smirk.
Her oval eyes like echoes
flooding with green

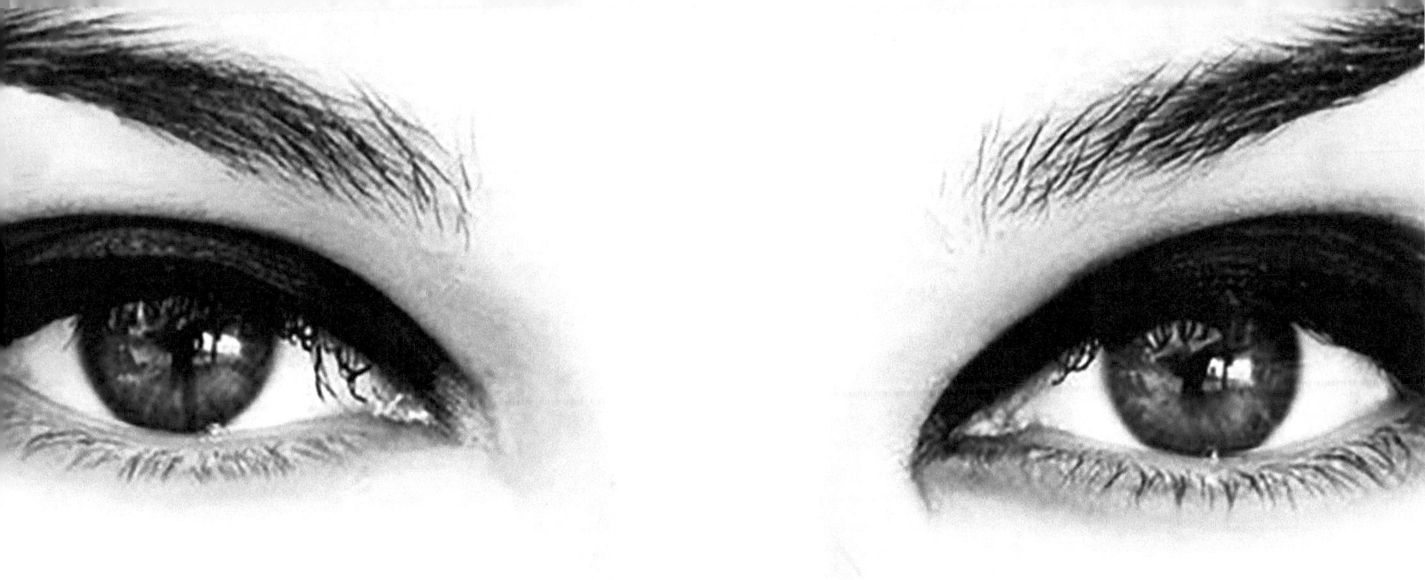

Two people
Debbie Tosun Kilday

Two bodies
Naked
Exposed
Two hearts
Beating
As one
Two lips
Locked
In a kiss
Two eyes
Viewing
The others soul
No status
No political affiliation
Nothing but...
Two people
At that moment
In time
Just two people
Nothing else

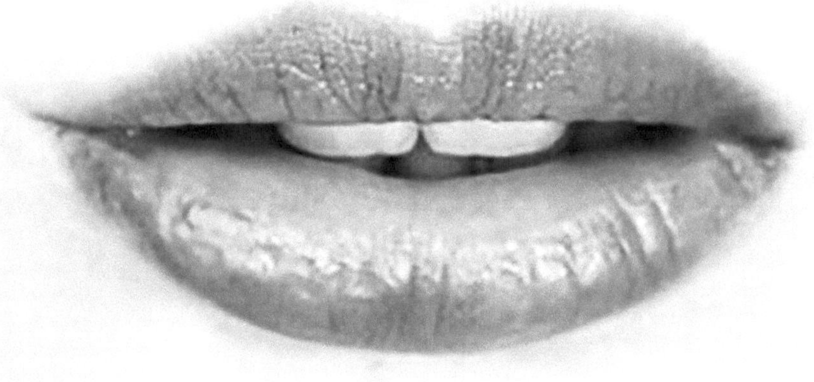

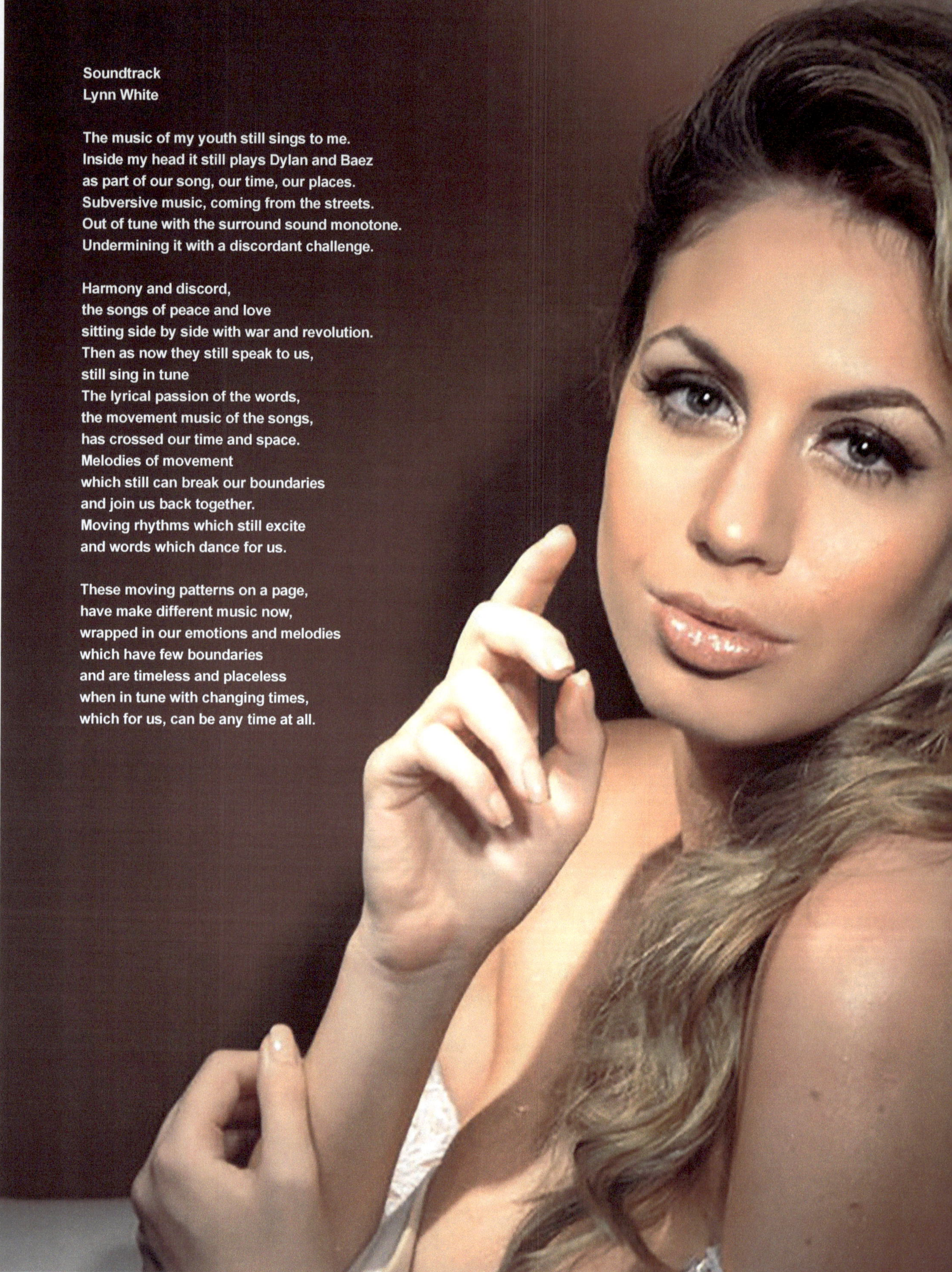

Soundtrack
Lynn White

The music of my youth still sings to me.
Inside my head it still plays Dylan and Baez
as part of our song, our time, our places.
Subversive music, coming from the streets.
Out of tune with the surround sound monotone.
Undermining it with a discordant challenge.

Harmony and discord,
the songs of peace and love
sitting side by side with war and revolution.
Then as now they still speak to us,
still sing in tune
The lyrical passion of the words,
the movement music of the songs,
has crossed our time and space.
Melodies of movement
which still can break our boundaries
and join us back together.
Moving rhythms which still excite
and words which dance for us.

These moving patterns on a page,
have make different music now,
wrapped in our emotions and melodies
which have few boundaries
and are timeless and placeless
when in tune with changing times,
which for us, can be any time at all.

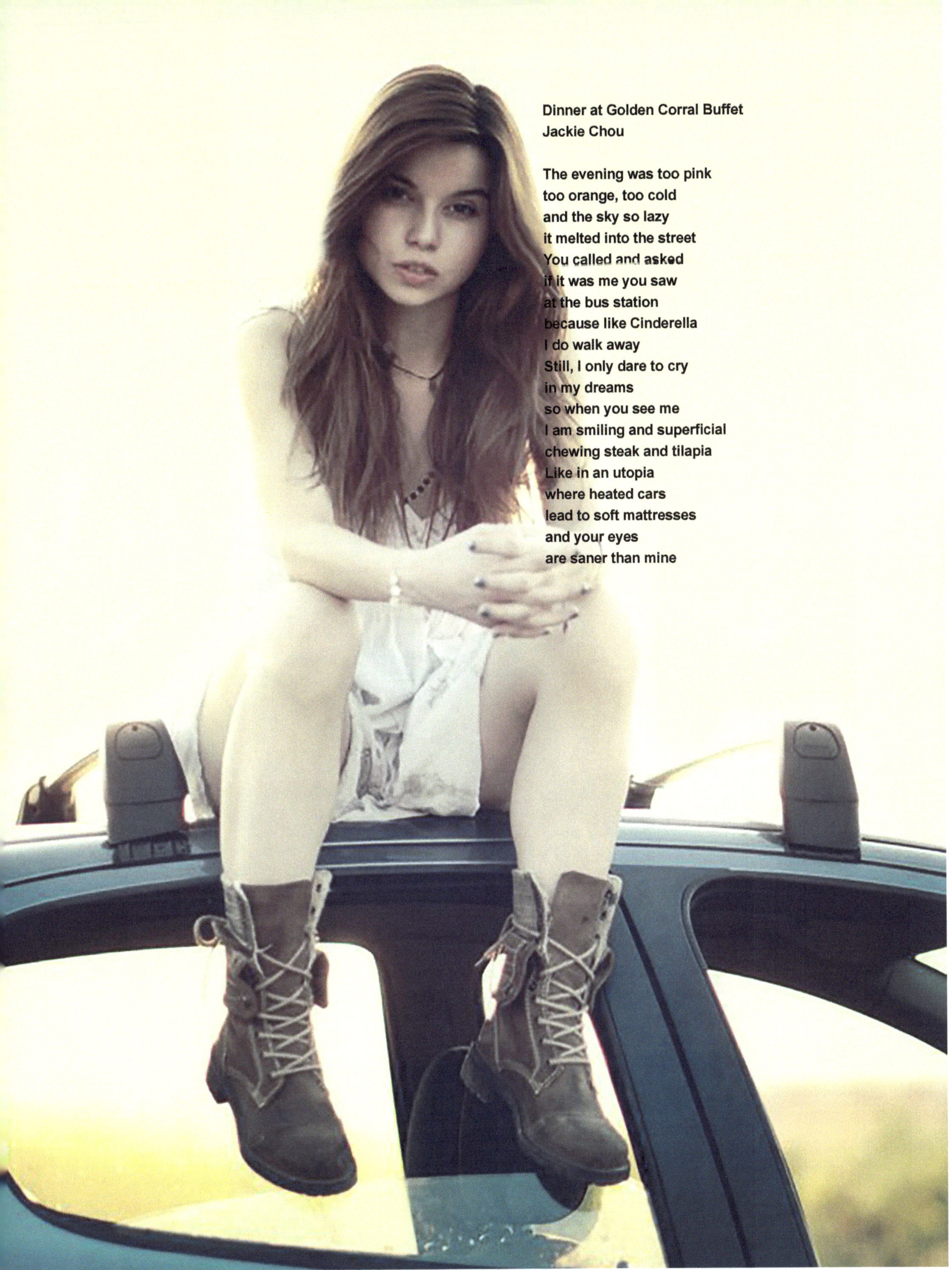

Dinner at Golden Corral Buffet
Jackie Chou

The evening was too pink
too orange, too cold
and the sky so lazy
it melted into the street
You called and asked
if it was me you saw
at the bus station
because like Cinderella
I do walk away
Still, I only dare to cry
in my dreams
so when you see me
I am smiling and superficial
chewing steak and tilapia
Like in an utopia
where heated cars
lead to soft mattresses
and your eyes
are saner than mine

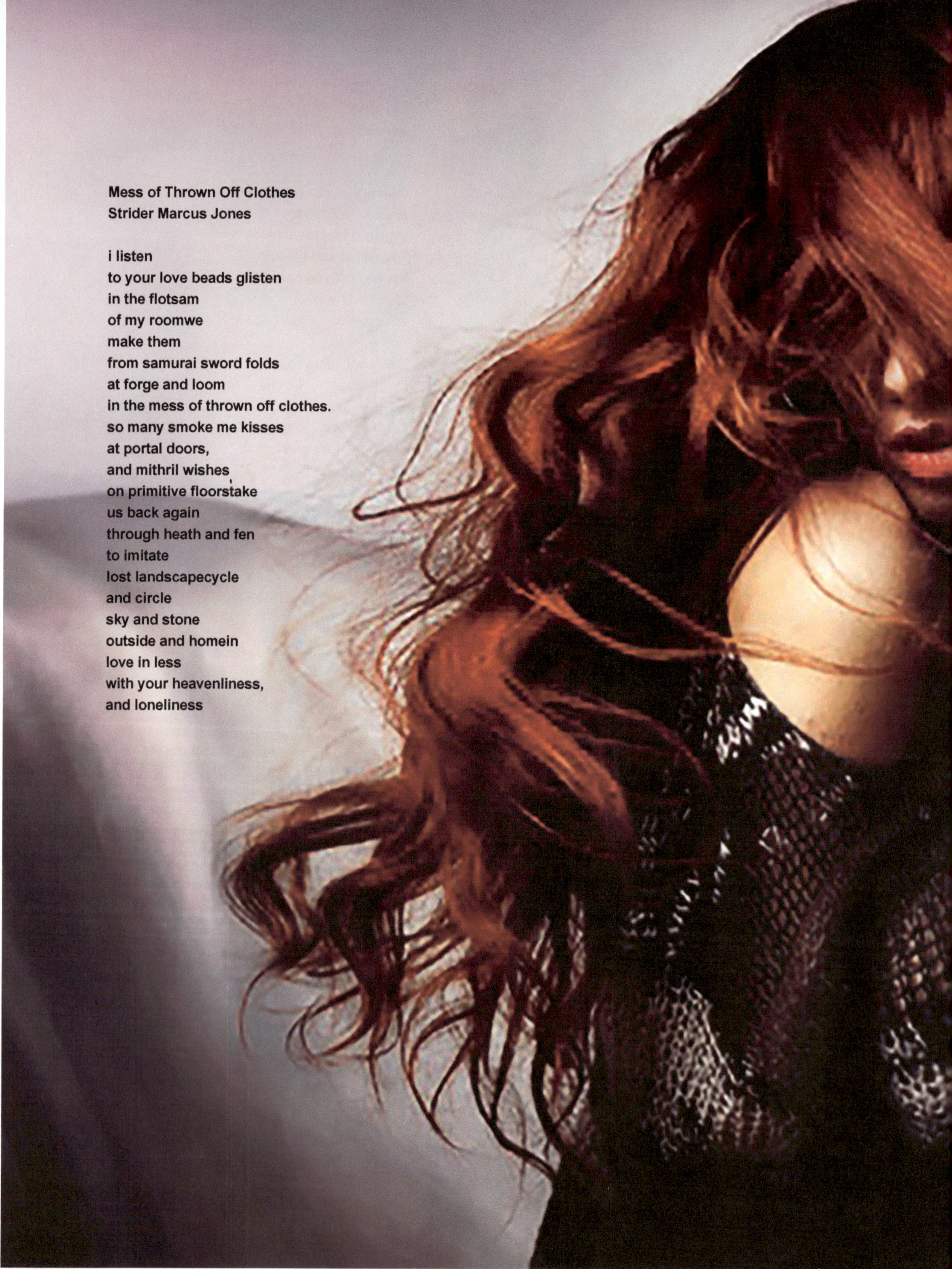

Mess of Thrown Off Clothes
Strider Marcus Jones

i listen
to your love beads glisten
in the flotsam
of my roomwe
make them
from samurai sword folds
at forge and loom
in the mess of thrown off clothes.
so many smoke me kisses
at portal doors,
and mithril wishes
on primitive floorstake
us back again
through heath and fen
to imitate
lost landscapecycle
and circle
sky and stone
outside and homein
love in less
with your heavenliness,
and loneliness

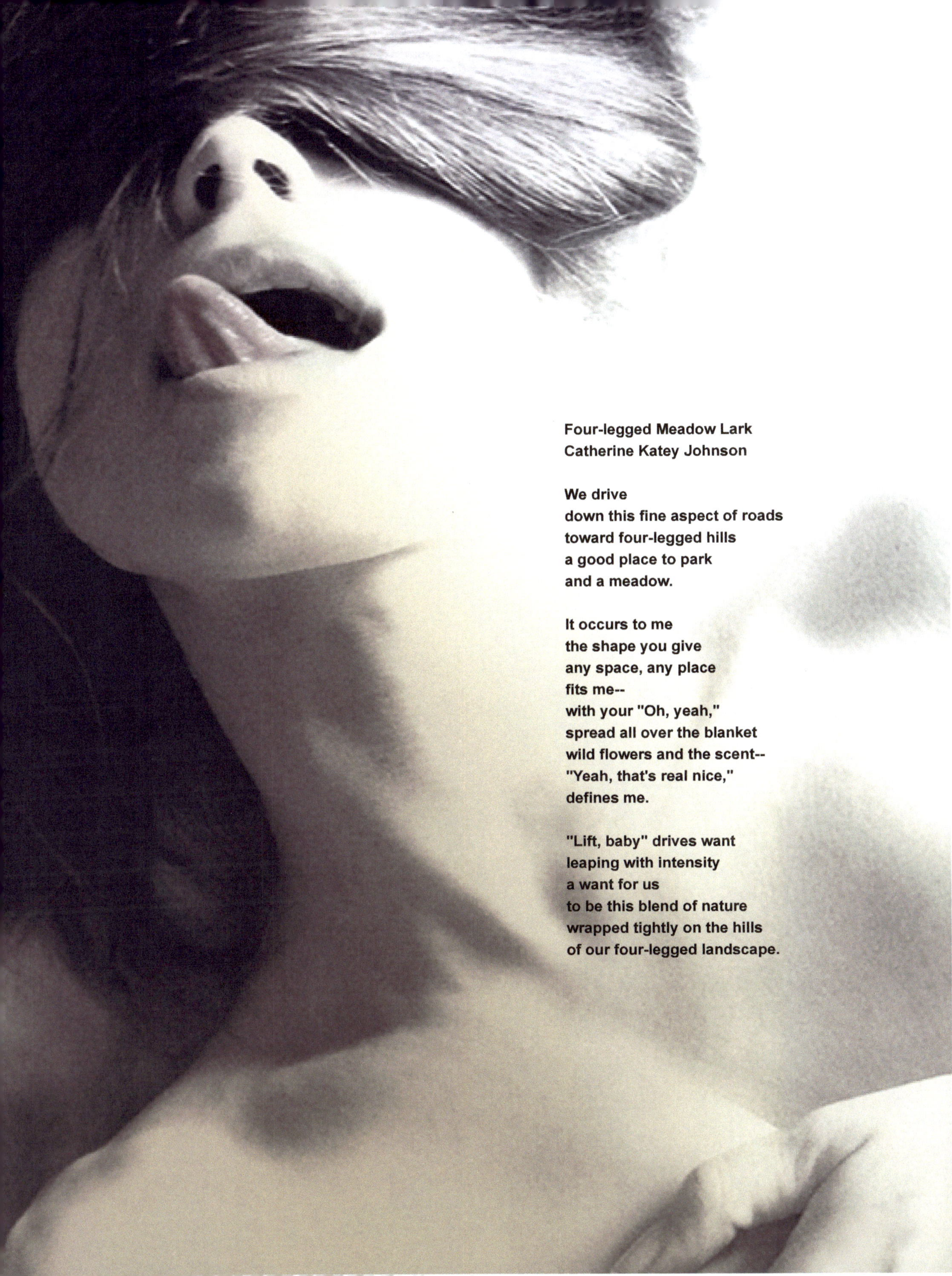

Four-legged Meadow Lark
Catherine Katey Johnson

We drive
down this fine aspect of roads
toward four-legged hills
a good place to park
and a meadow.

It occurs to me
the shape you give
any space, any place
fits me--
with your "Oh, yeah,"
spread all over the blanket
wild flowers and the scent--
"Yeah, that's real nice,"
defines me.

"Lift, baby" drives want
leaping with intensity
a want for us
to be this blend of nature
wrapped tightly on the hills
of our four-legged landscape.

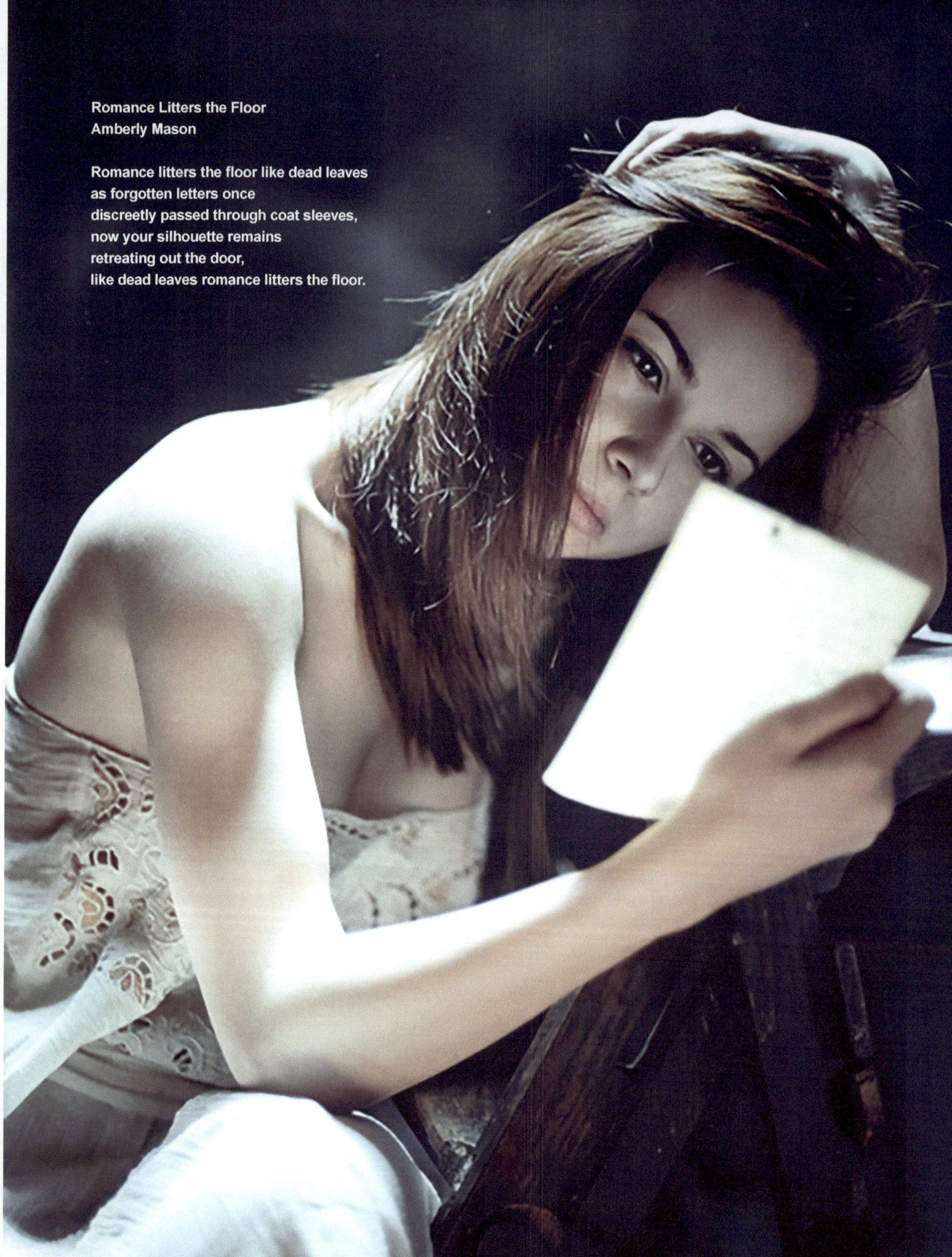
Romance Litters the Floor
Amberly Mason

Romance litters the floor like dead leaves
as forgotten letters once
discreetly passed through coat sleeves,
now your silhouette remains
retreating out the door,
like dead leaves romance litters the floor.

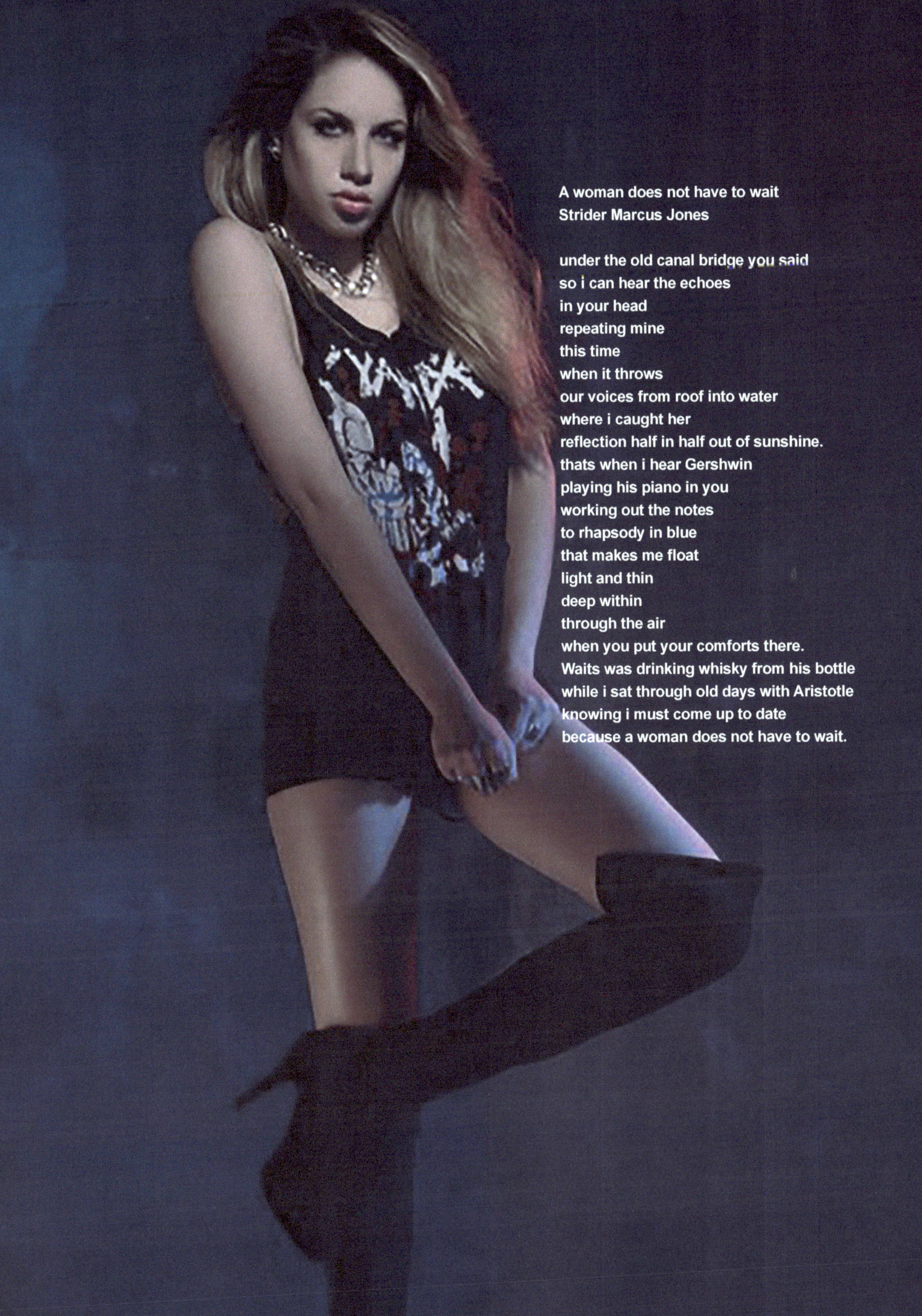
A woman does not have to wait
Strider Marcus Jones

under the old canal bridge you said
so i can hear the echoes
in your head
repeating mine
this time
when it throws
our voices from roof into water
where i caught her
reflection half in half out of sunshine.
thats when i hear Gershwin
playing his piano in you
working out the notes
to rhapsody in blue
that makes me float
light and thin
deep within
through the air
when you put your comforts there.
Waits was drinking whisky from his bottle
while i sat through old days with Aristotle
knowing i must come up to date
because a woman does not have to wait.

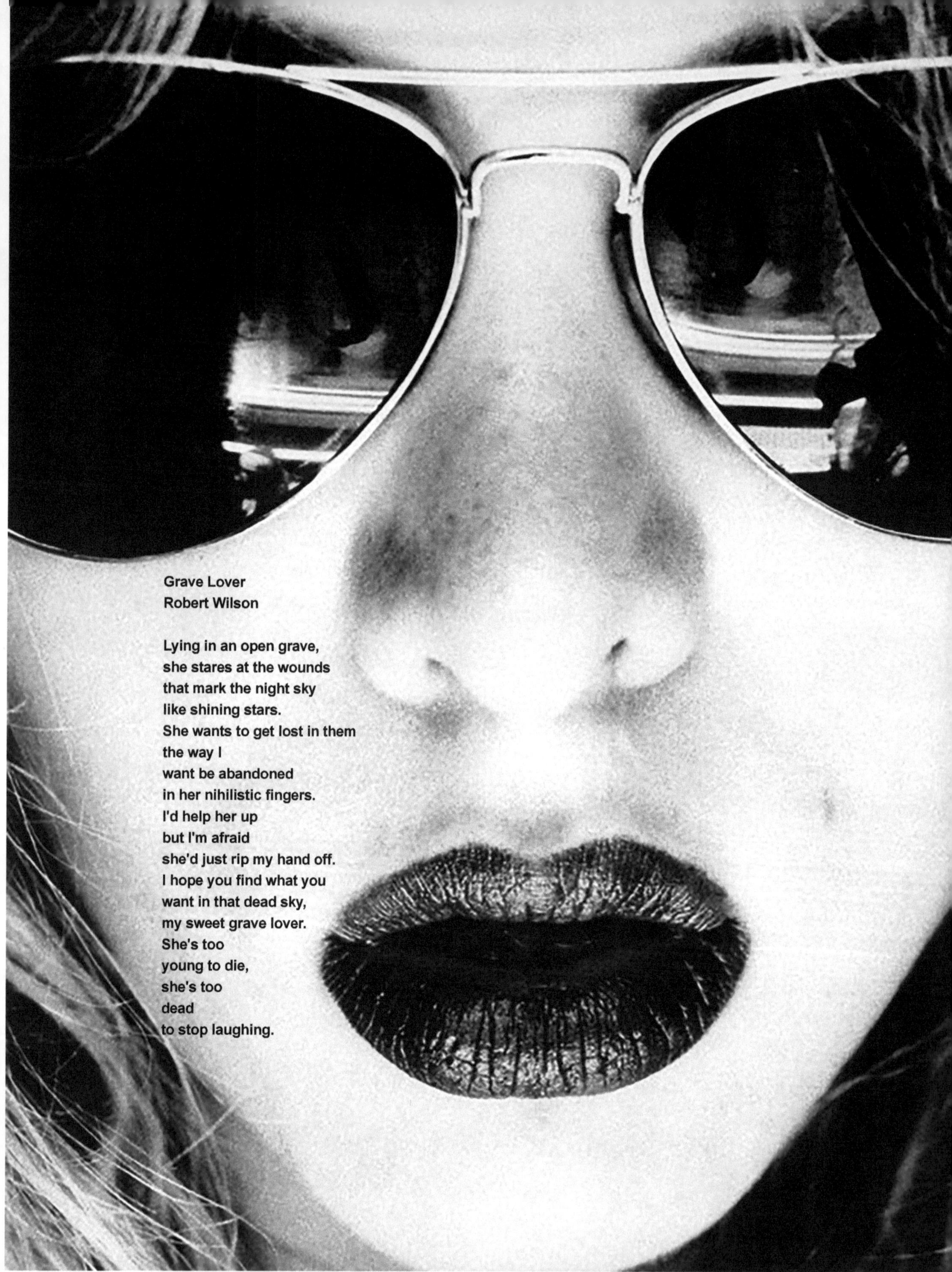

Grave Lover
Robert Wilson

Lying in an open grave,
she stares at the wounds
that mark the night sky
like shining stars.
She wants to get lost in them
the way I
want be abandoned
in her nihilistic fingers.
I'd help her up
but I'm afraid
she'd just rip my hand off.
I hope you find what you
want in that dead sky,
my sweet grave lover.
She's too
young to die,
she's too
dead
to stop laughing.

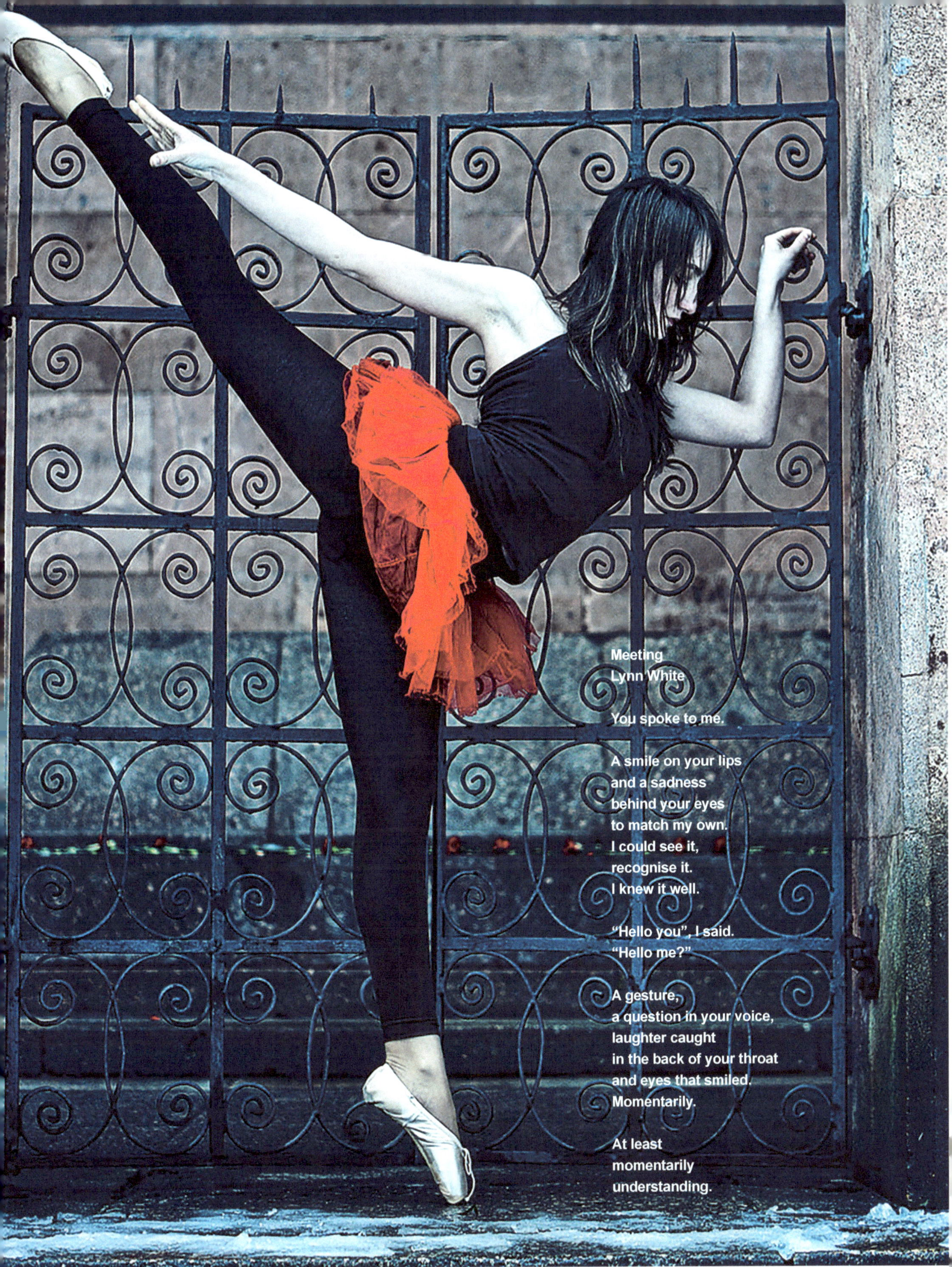

Meeting
Lynn White

You spoke to me.

A smile on your lips
and a sadness
behind your eyes
to match my own.
I could see it,
recognise it.
I knew it well.

"Hello you", I said.
"Hello me?"

A gesture,
a question in your voice,
laughter caught
in the back of your throat
and eyes that smiled.
Momentarily.

At least
momentarily
understanding.

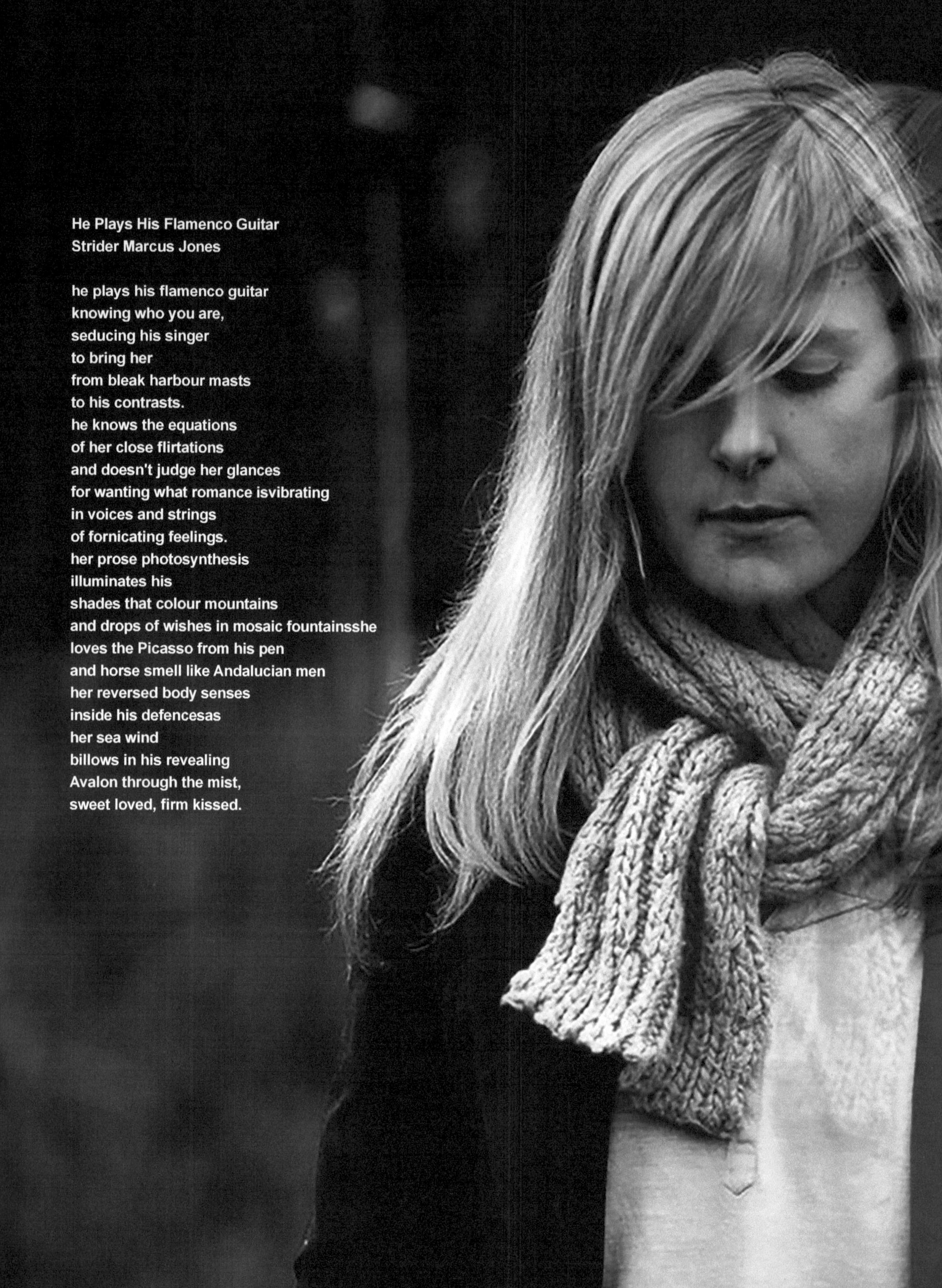

He Plays His Flamenco Guitar
Strider Marcus Jones

he plays his flamenco guitar
knowing who you are,
seducing his singer
to bring her
from bleak harbour masts
to his contrasts.
he knows the equations
of her close flirtations
and doesn't judge her glances
for wanting what romance isvibrating
in voices and strings
of fornicating feelings.
her prose photosynthesis
illuminates his
shades that colour mountains
and drops of wishes in mosaic fountainsshe
loves the Picasso from his pen
and horse smell like Andalucian men
her reversed body senses
inside his defencesas
her sea wind
billows in his revealing
Avalon through the mist,
sweet loved, firm kissed.

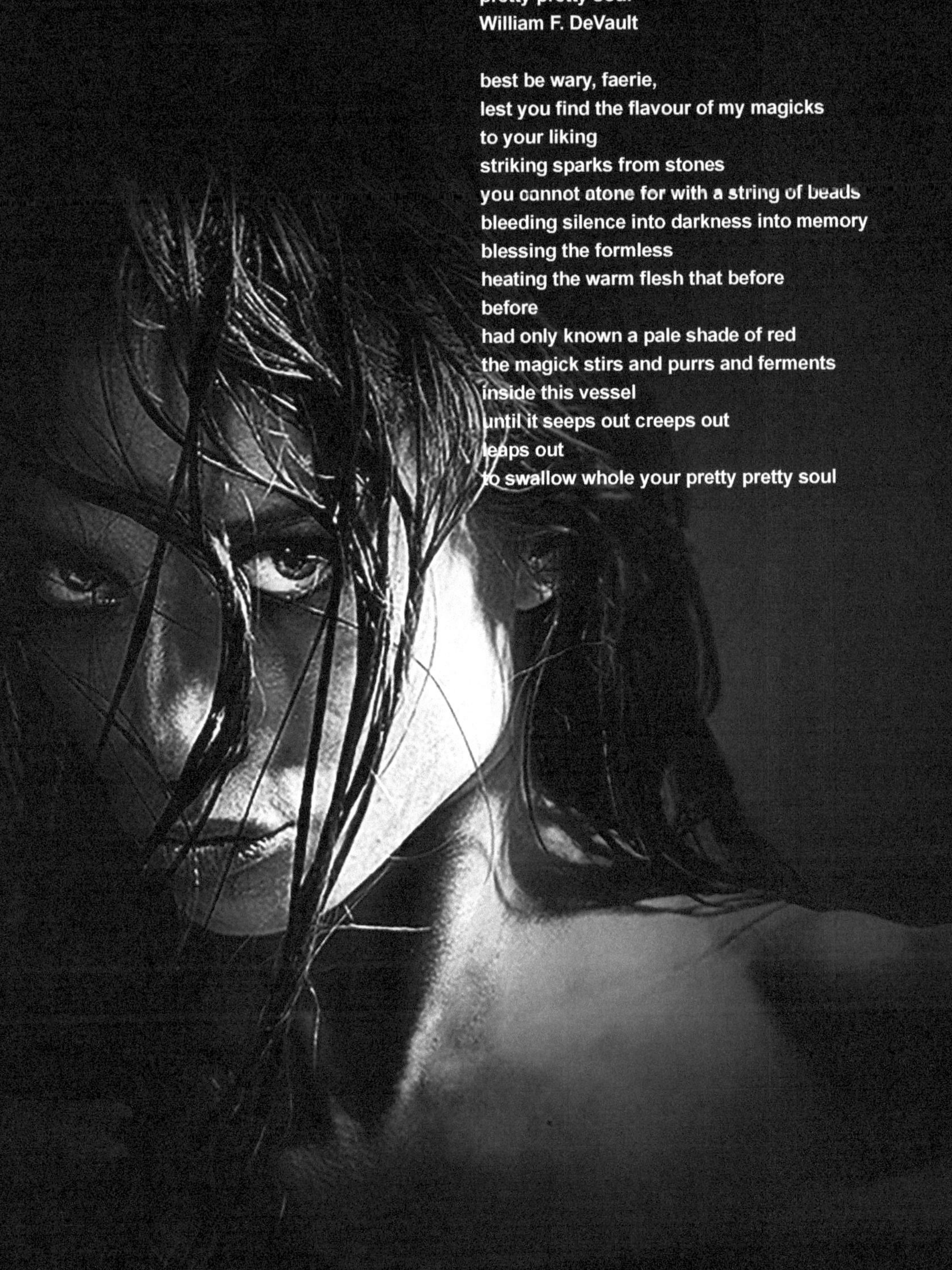

pretty pretty soul
William F. DeVault

best be wary, faerie,
lest you find the flavour of my magicks
to your liking
striking sparks from stones
you cannot atone for with a string of beads
bleeding silence into darkness into memory
blessing the formless
heating the warm flesh that before
before
had only known a pale shade of red
the magick stirs and purrs and ferments
inside this vessel
until it seeps out creeps out
leaps out
to swallow whole your pretty pretty soul

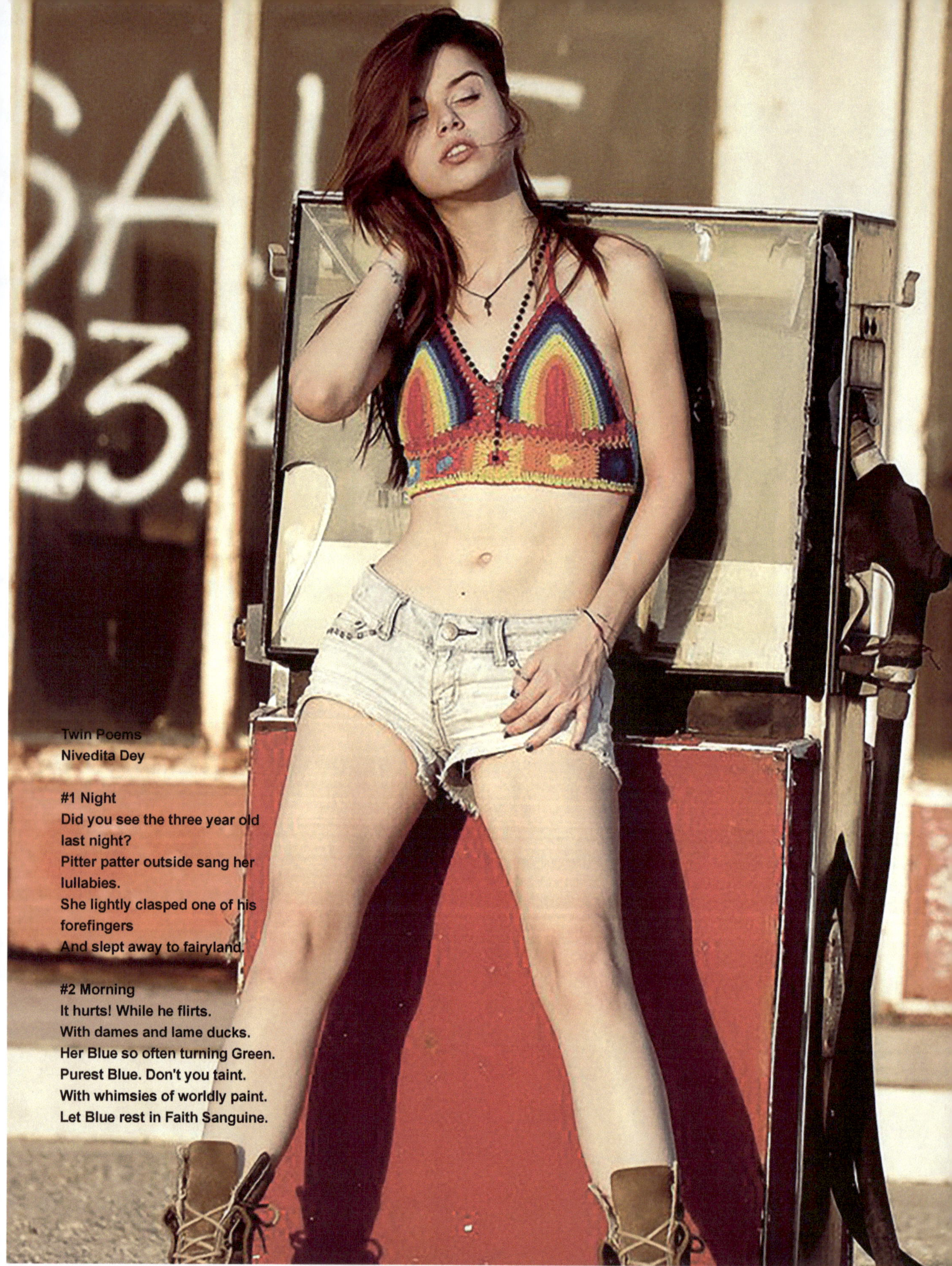

Twin Poems
Nivedita Dey

#1 Night
Did you see the three year old
last night?
Pitter patter outside sang her
lullabies.
She lightly clasped one of his
forefingers
And slept away to fairyland.

#2 Morning
It hurts! While he flirts.
With dames and lame ducks.
Her Blue so often turning Green.
Purest Blue. Don't you taint.
With whimsies of worldly paint.
Let Blue rest in Faith Sanguine.

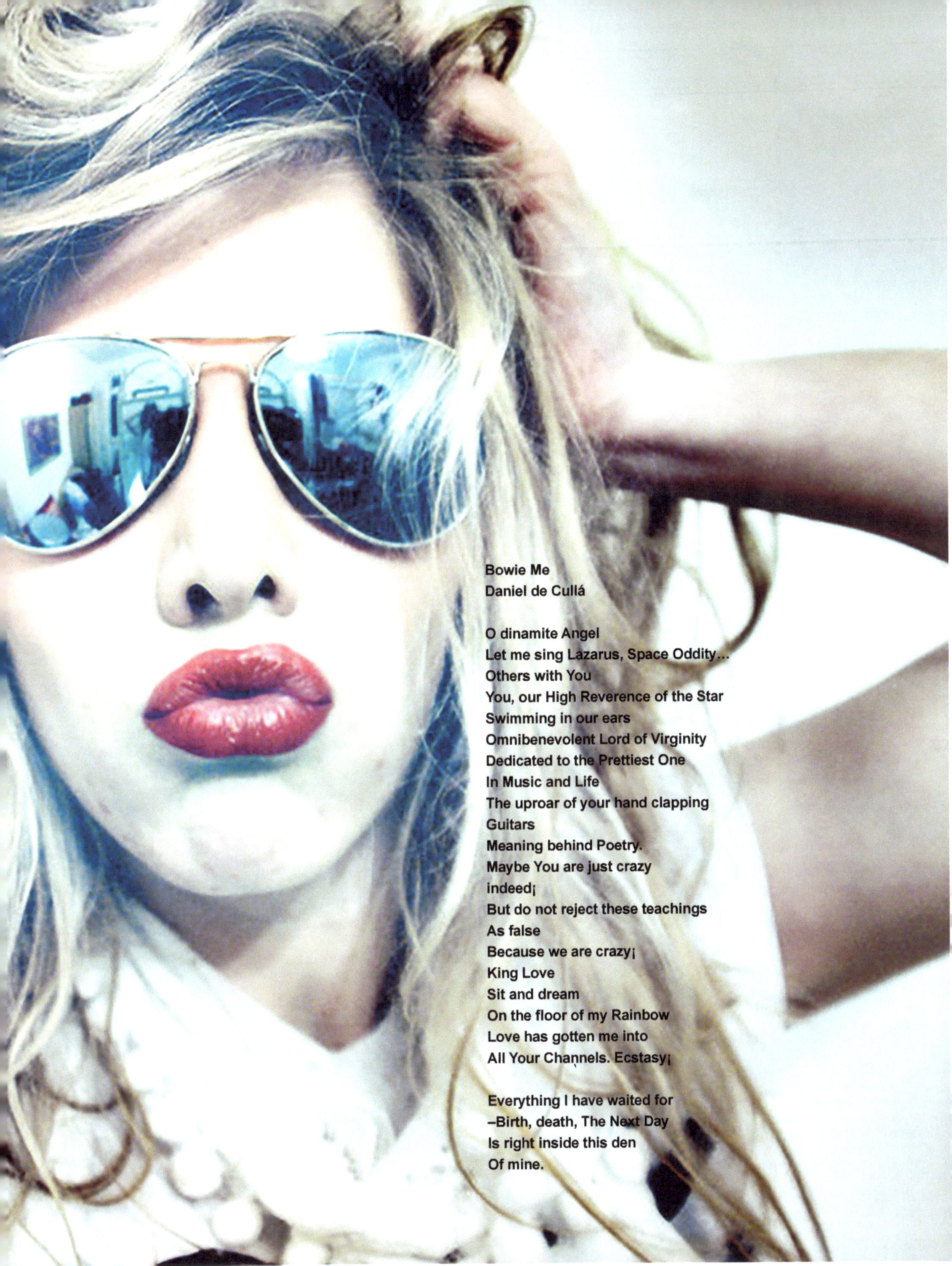

Bowie Me
Daniel de Cullá

O dinamite Angel
Let me sing Lazarus, Space Oddity…
Others with You
You, our High Reverence of the Star
Swimming in our ears
Omnibenevolent Lord of Virginity
Dedicated to the Prettiest One
In Music and Life
The uproar of your hand clapping
Guitars
Meaning behind Poetry.
Maybe You are just crazy
indeed¡
But do not reject these teachings
As false
Because we are crazy¡
King Love
Sit and dream
On the floor of my Rainbow
Love has gotten me into
All Your Channels. Ecstasy¡

Everything I have waited for
—Birth, death, The Next Day
Is right inside this den
Of mine.

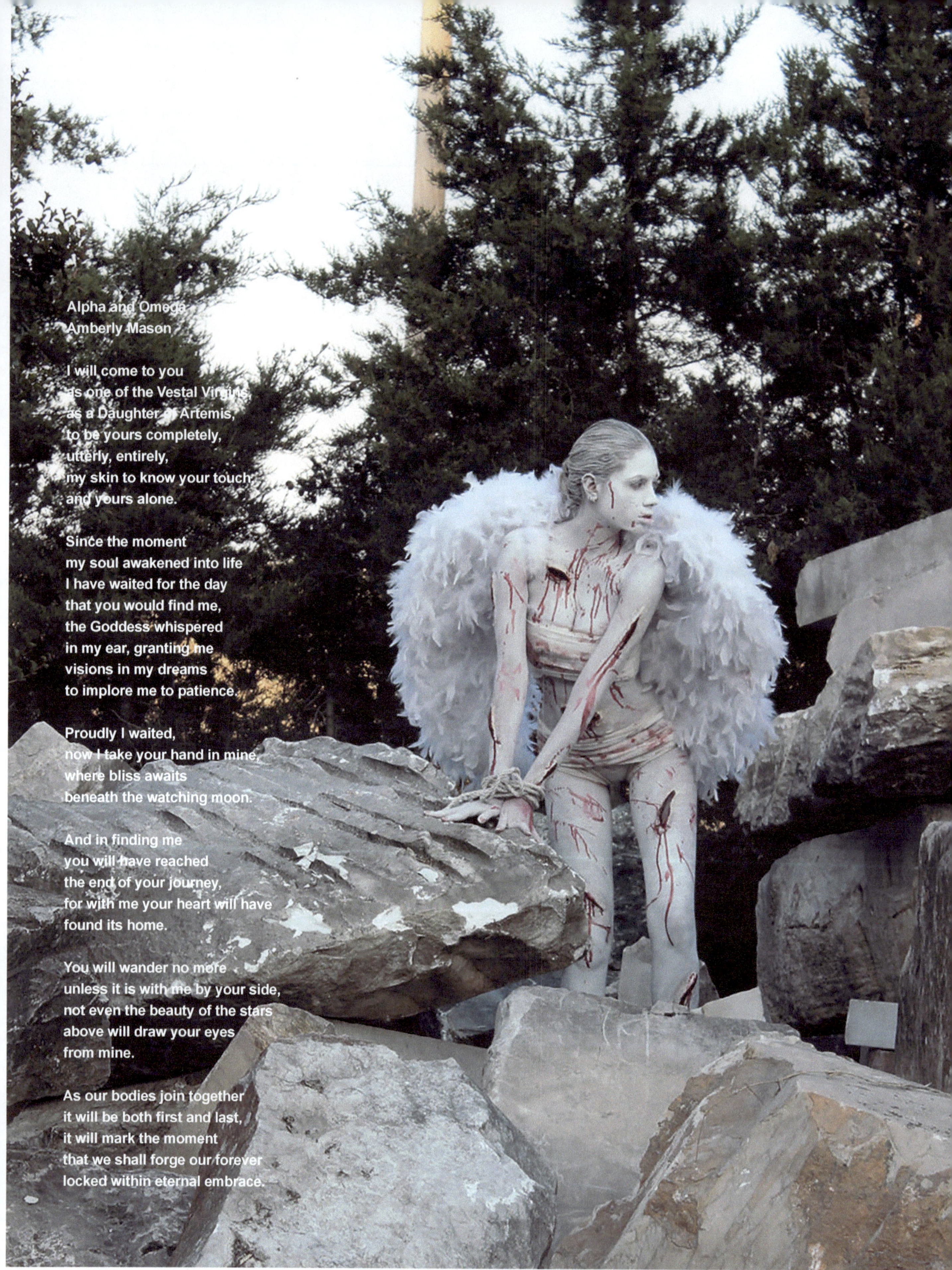

Alpha and Omega
Amberly Mason

I will come to you
as one of the Vestal Virgins,
as a Daughter of Artemis,
to be yours completely,
utterly, entirely,
my skin to know your touch
and yours alone.

Since the moment
my soul awakened into life
I have waited for the day
that you would find me,
the Goddess whispered
in my ear, granting me
visions in my dreams
to implore me to patience.

Proudly I waited,
now I take your hand in mine,
where bliss awaits
beneath the watching moon.

And in finding me
you will have reached
the end of your journey,
for with me your heart will have
found its home.

You will wander no more
unless it is with me by your side,
not even the beauty of the stars
above will draw your eyes
from mine.

As our bodies join together
it will be both first and last,
it will mark the moment
that we shall forge our forever
locked within eternal embrace.

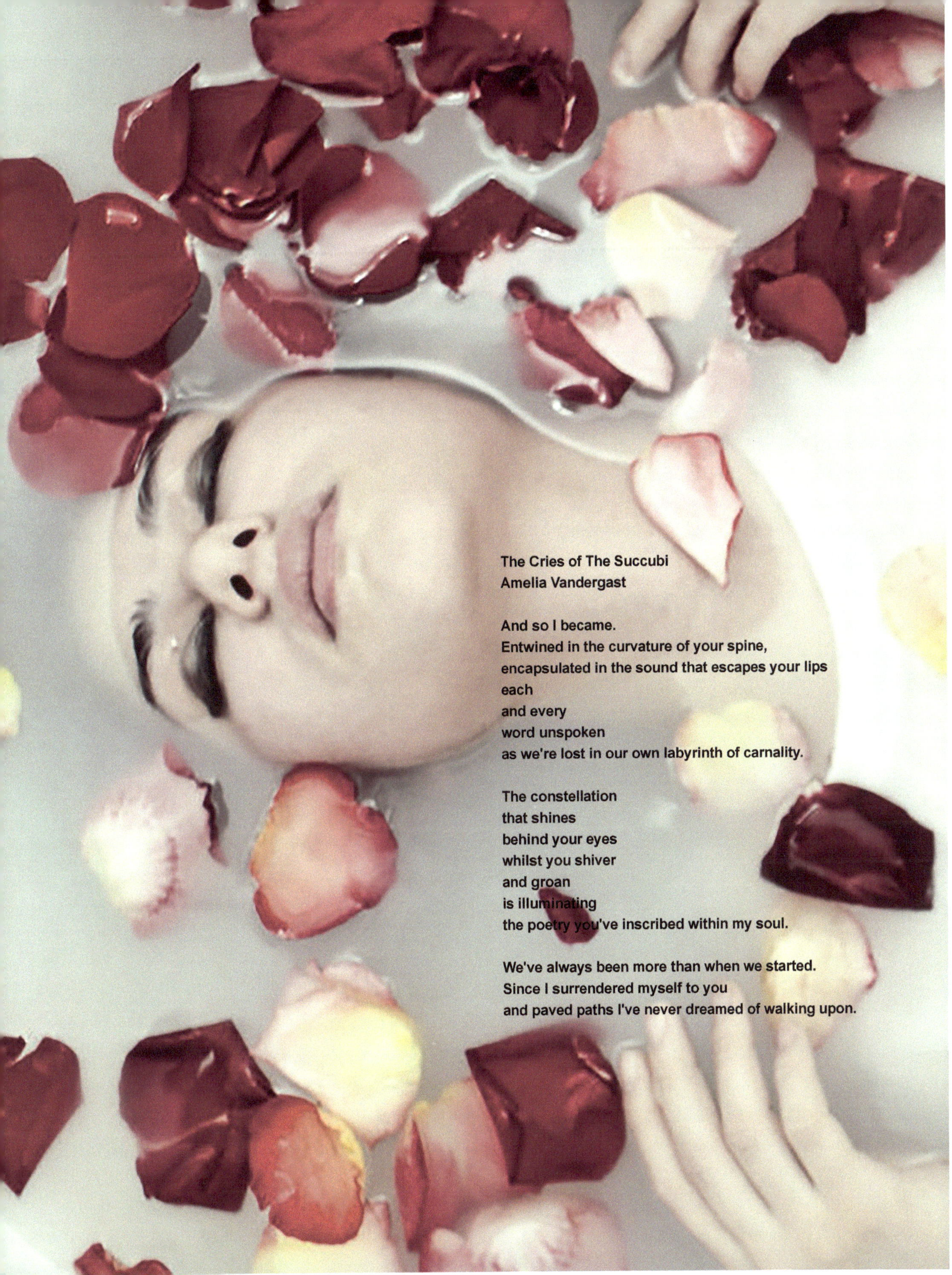

The Cries of The Succubi
Amelia Vandergast

And so I became.
Entwined in the curvature of your spine,
encapsulated in the sound that escapes your lips
each
and every
word unspoken
as we're lost in our own labyrinth of carnality.

The constellation
that shines
behind your eyes
whilst you shiver
and groan
is illuminating
the poetry you've inscribed within my soul.

We've always been more than when we started.
Since I surrendered myself to you
and paved paths I've never dreamed of walking upon.

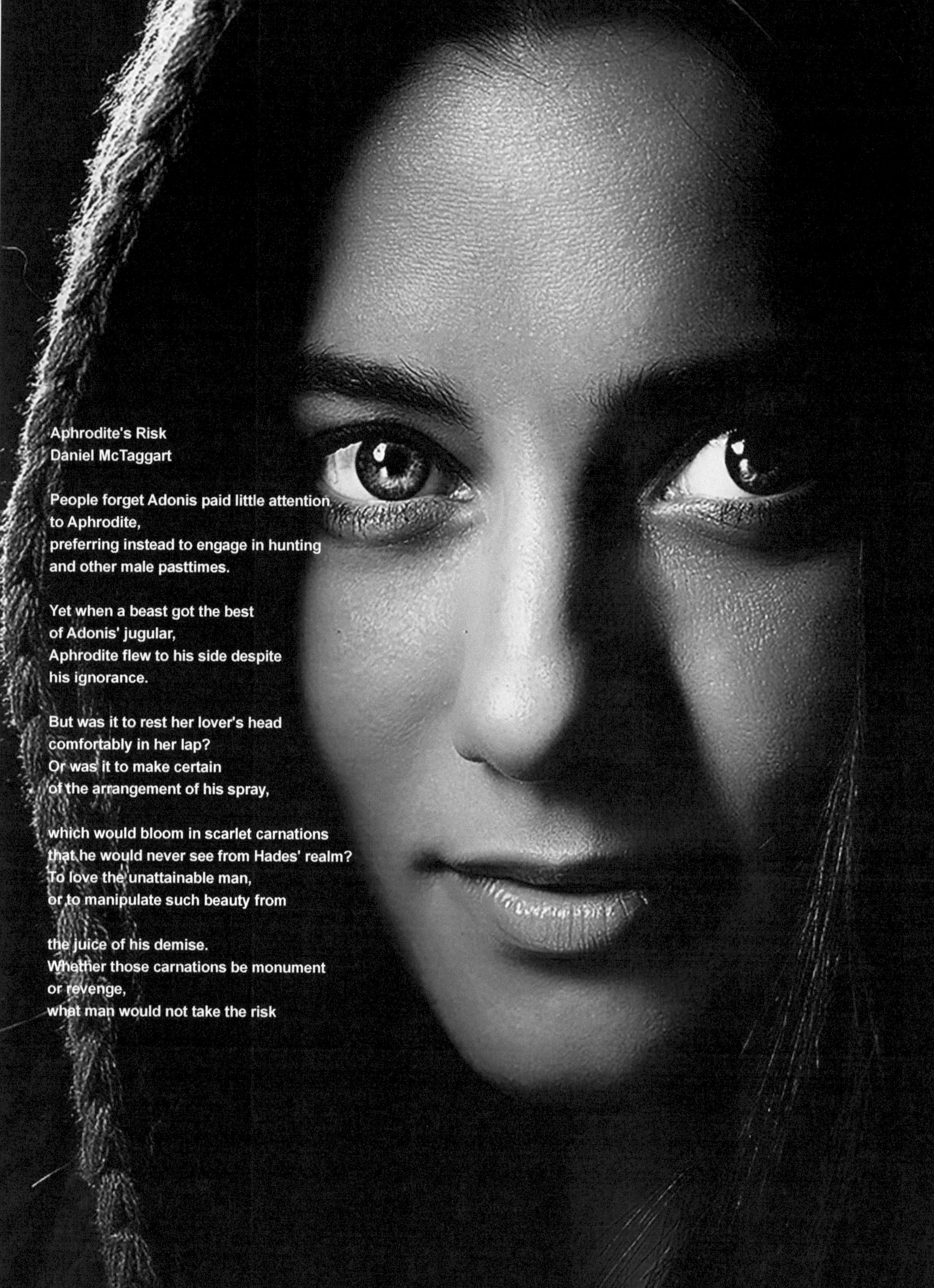
Aphrodite's Risk
Daniel McTaggart

People forget Adonis paid little attention
to Aphrodite,
preferring instead to engage in hunting
and other male pasttimes.

Yet when a beast got the best
of Adonis' jugular,
Aphrodite flew to his side despite
his ignorance.

But was it to rest her lover's head
comfortably in her lap?
Or was it to make certain
of the arrangement of his spray,

which would bloom in scarlet carnations
that he would never see from Hades' realm?
To love the unattainable man,
or to manipulate such beauty from

the juice of his demise.
Whether those carnations be monument
or revenge,
what man would not take the risk

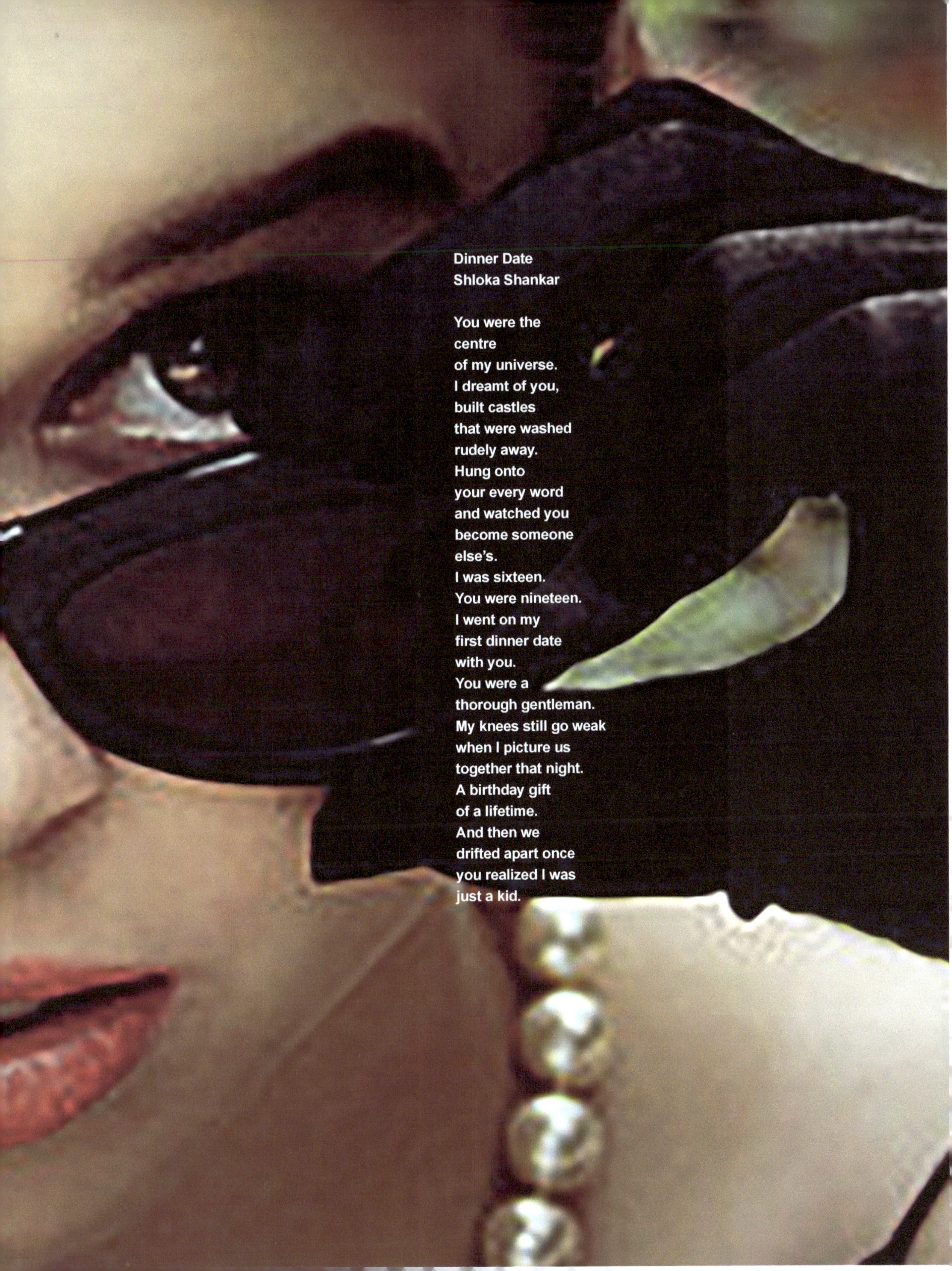

Dinner Date
Shloka Shankar

You were the
centre
of my universe.
I dreamt of you,
built castles
that were washed
rudely away.
Hung onto
your every word
and watched you
become someone
else's.
I was sixteen.
You were nineteen.
I went on my
first dinner date
with you.
You were a
thorough gentleman.
My knees still go weak
when I picture us
together that night.
A birthday gift
of a lifetime.
And then we
drifted apart once
you realized I was
just a kid.

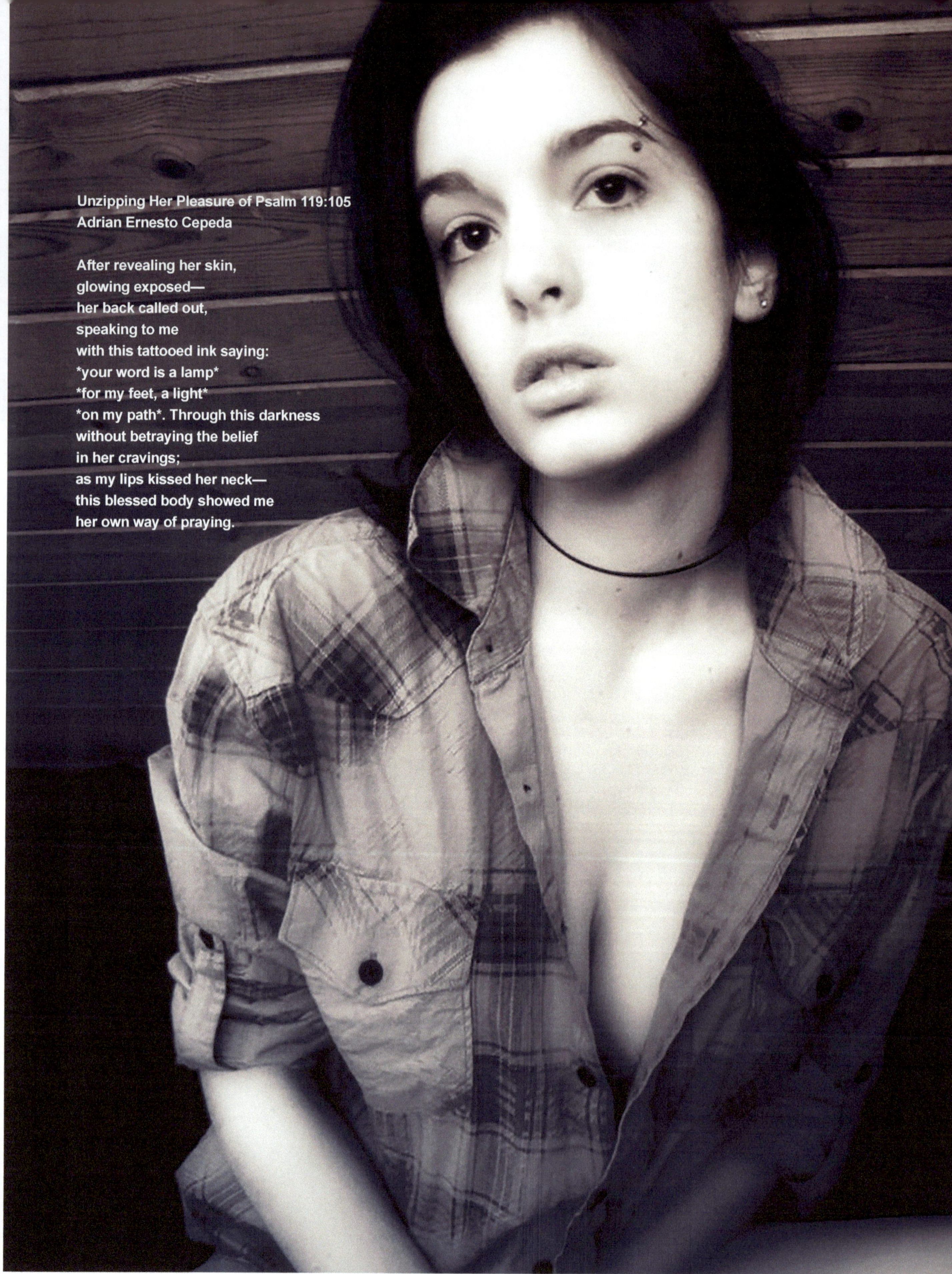

Unzipping Her Pleasure of Psalm 119:105
Adrian Ernesto Cepeda

After revealing her skin,
glowing exposed—
her back called out,
speaking to me
with this tattooed ink saying:
your word is a lamp
for my feet, a light
on my path. Through this darkness
without betraying the belief
in her cravings;
as my lips kissed her neck—
this blessed body showed me
her own way of praying.

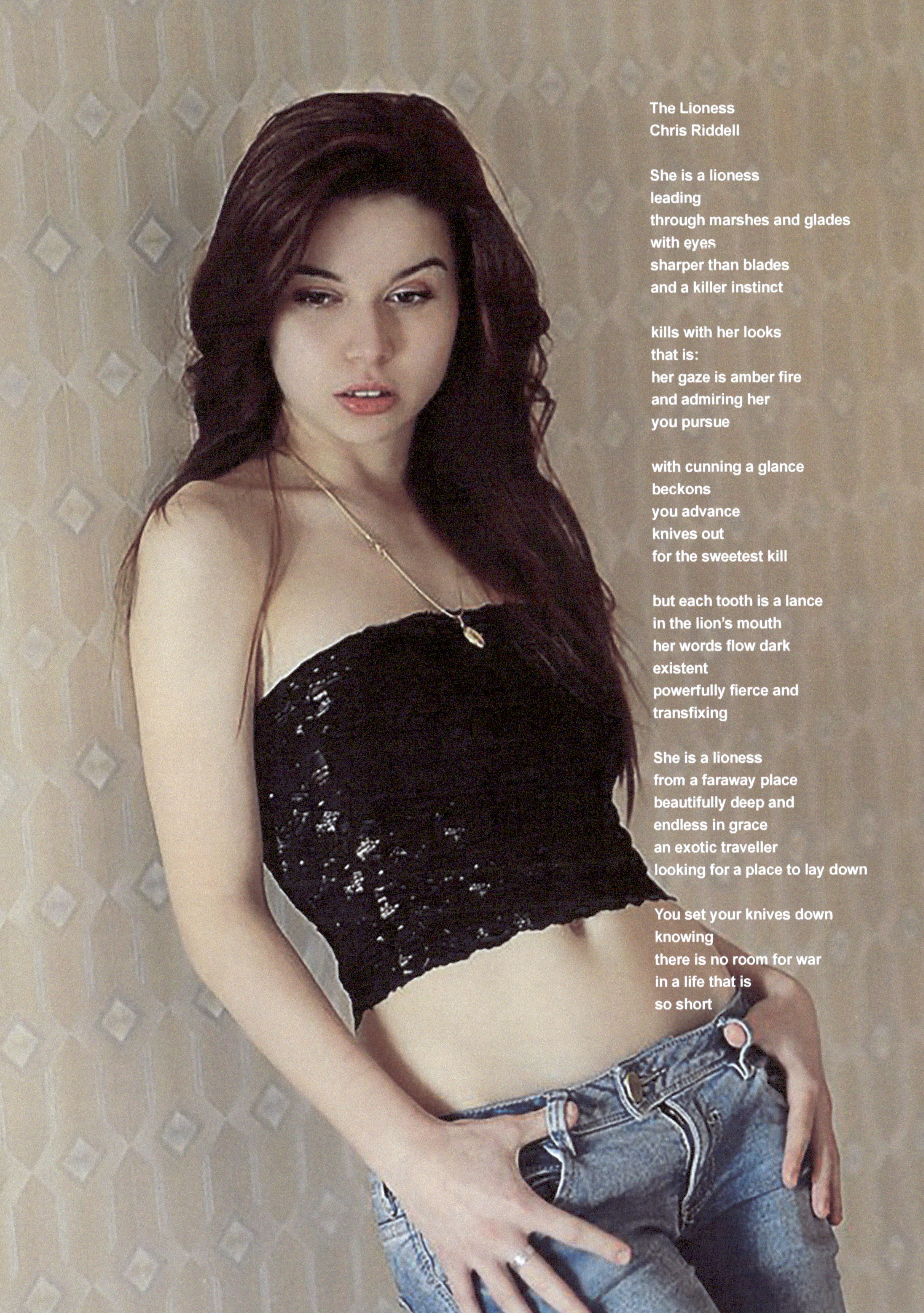

The Lioness
Chris Riddell

She is a lioness
leading
through marshes and glades
with eyes
sharper than blades
and a killer instinct

kills with her looks
that is:
her gaze is amber fire
and admiring her
you pursue

with cunning a glance
beckons
you advance
knives out
for the sweetest kill

but each tooth is a lance
in the lion's mouth
her words flow dark
existent
powerfully fierce and
transfixing

She is a lioness
from a faraway place
beautifully deep and
endless in grace
an exotic traveller
looking for a place to lay down

You set your knives down
knowing
there is no room for war
in a life that is
so short

An American Night
Daniel McTaggart

I'm going out for a burger fried on the grill
with black lines searing across the patty,
like prison bars holding juices in,
letting them out on good behavior as I bite.

I want it thick enough to be pink in the middle.
I want a strawberry shake so thick
I have to eat it with a spoon.

I want fries the size of my fingers.
I want them to burn my tongue with every bite.
And if they sizzle in my hand before I do,
that will be just fine.

I will put a quarter in the juke box
and play "Sugar Shack" by Jimmy Gilmer
because "there's a cute li'l girlie who's
a-workin' there. In black leotards
and her feet are bare."

I will go to the coffee shop and drink
a blend so rich and so full
I might stay up for a week.

I will walk in fields up to my neck in grass
side by side with an American girl,
her hair so long and her skirt so short
they meet each other at mid-thigh.

Her father won't know where we are.
And we won't care because we've found
the perfect place to lie back
and look up at stars.

We will count constellations in lieu of
counting down the moments till our first time.
Our first time together, which will be
somewhere between the Big Dipper
and the belt of Orion.

Then I will take her home, climbing up
behind her to the second story window.
Begging to stay when I know I can't.
Leaving before her father finds out.

I'll wish I could stick around,
like John Belushi on a ladder,
but I will respect her.

She will flop on her bed, dreaming
all the ways this night could
not have gone better.

Twirling a lock of hair with one hand.
Caressing her lips with the other.
Praying for my next phone call.
Hoping for another second story rendezvous.

I will dream only of her
and how she moved beneath me.
How stars whistled through reeds
to settle in the corners of her eyes.

Tomorrow morning, while I eat breakfast,
Mom will hold my jeans above the washer
like a painting, wondering how I got
such dark grass stains in the knees.

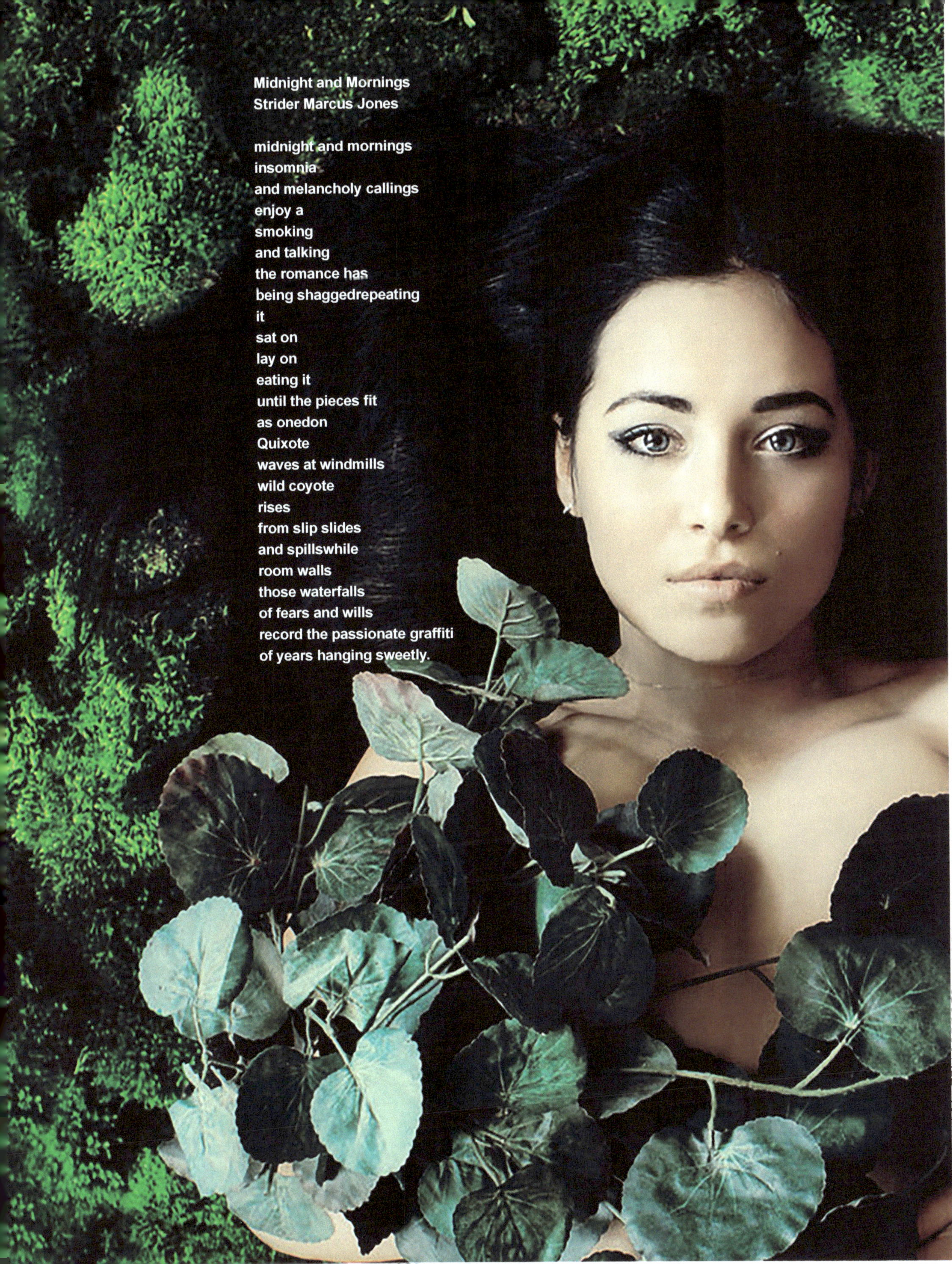

Midnight and Mornings
Strider Marcus Jones

midnight and mornings
insomnia
and melancholy callings
enjoy a
smoking
and talking
the romance has
being shaggedrepeating
it
sat on
lay on
eating it
until the pieces fit
as onedon
Quixote
waves at windmills
wild coyote
rises
from slip slides
and spillswhile
room walls
those waterfalls
of fears and wills
record the passionate graffiti
of years hanging sweetly.

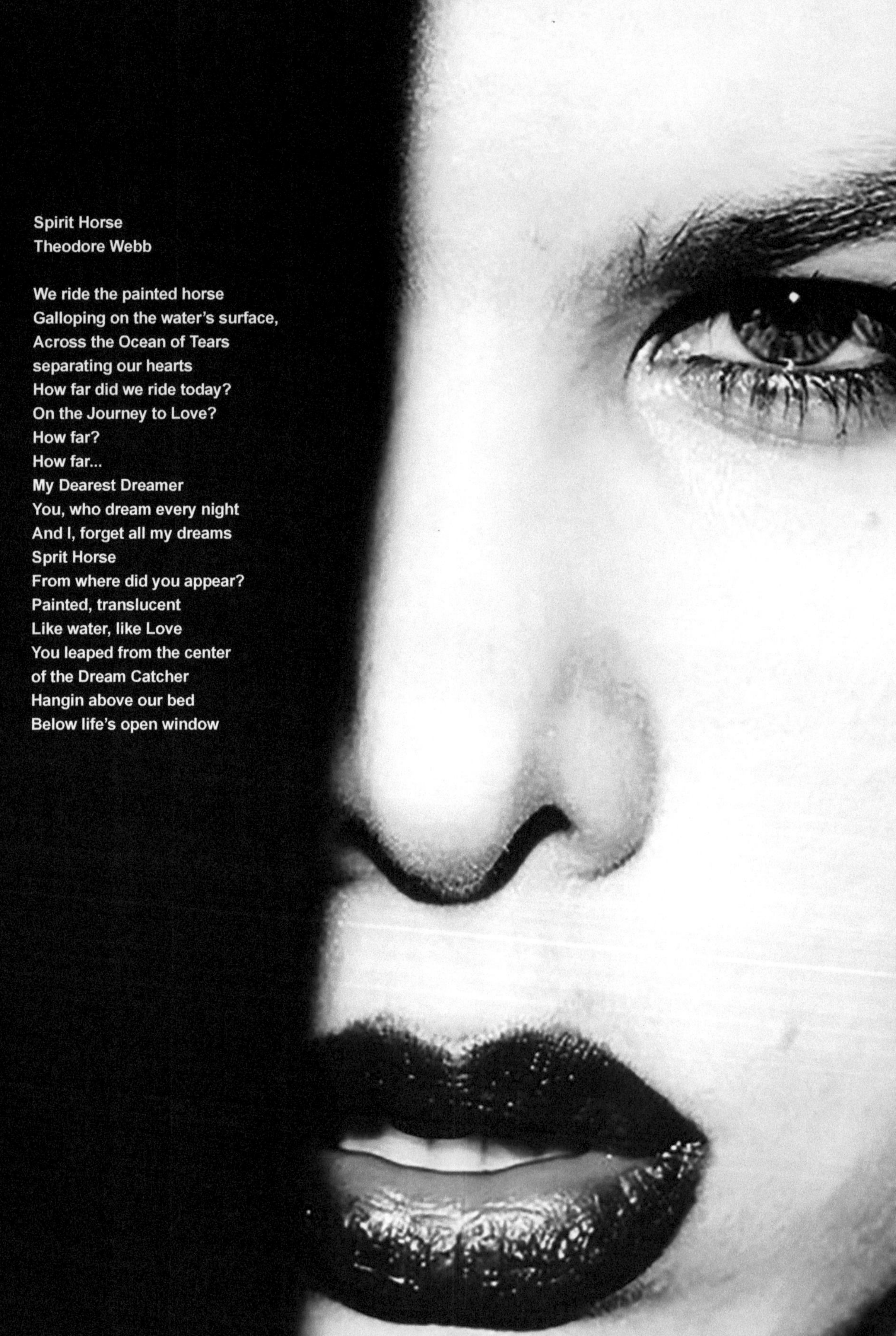

Spirit Horse
Theodore Webb

We ride the painted horse
Galloping on the water's surface,
Across the Ocean of Tears
separating our hearts
How far did we ride today?
On the Journey to Love?
How far?
How far...
My Dearest Dreamer
You, who dream every night
And I, forget all my dreams
Sprit Horse
From where did you appear?
Painted, translucent
Like water, like Love
You leaped from the center
of the Dream Catcher
Hangin above our bed
Below life's open window

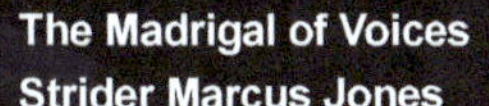

The Madrigal of Voices
Strider Marcus Jones

the madrigal of voices
somewhere, in its choices,
chooses and rejoices
back to me collecting
frozen wood,
from the crofts and slums, of old childhood
sat
here, on this chair
in the numb night air.
now, your moonbeams kiss
the winter of me. stirs
ripples on its pond skin. unpicks the threaded
wish
of passions positive remark
while
sleep fights
these luminous lights
of limp daggers laughing
in the dark.
somehow, its root
of subdued jasmine and tropical jute,
reaches that closed chamber of your core
and
thoughts transmute,
woven to the nature of its lore.
negativity narrows
when i stroke in your shallows
forward
as before;
but staying in tomorrows,
i enter and endure.

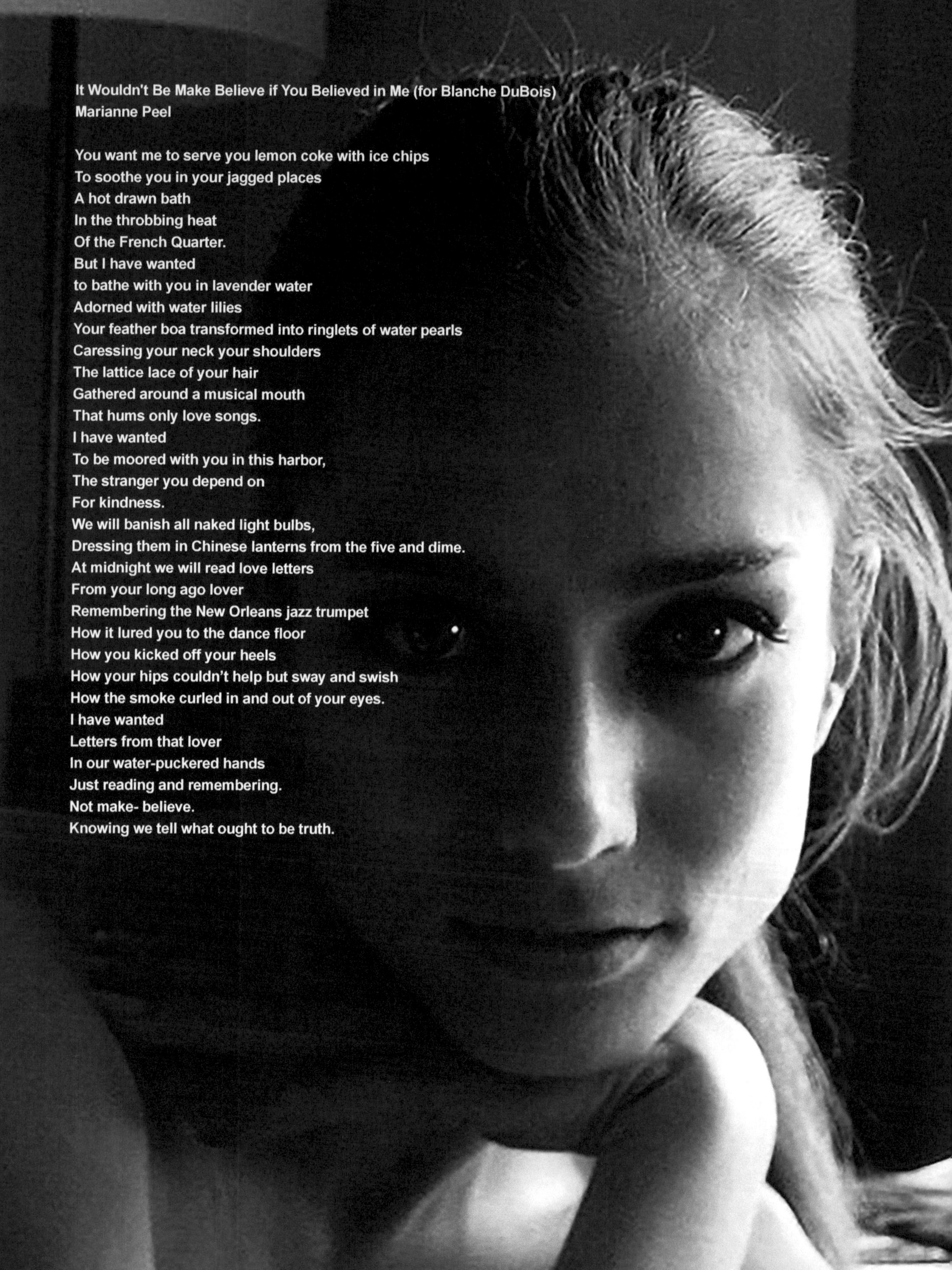

It Wouldn't Be Make Believe if You Believed in Me (for Blanche DuBois)
Marianne Peel

You want me to serve you lemon coke with ice chips
To soothe you in your jagged places
A hot drawn bath
In the throbbing heat
Of the French Quarter.
But I have wanted
to bathe with you in lavender water
Adorned with water lilies
Your feather boa transformed into ringlets of water pearls
Caressing your neck your shoulders
The lattice lace of your hair
Gathered around a musical mouth
That hums only love songs.
I have wanted
To be moored with you in this harbor,
The stranger you depend on
For kindness.
We will banish all naked light bulbs,
Dressing them in Chinese lanterns from the five and dime.
At midnight we will read love letters
From your long ago lover
Remembering the New Orleans jazz trumpet
How it lured you to the dance floor
How you kicked off your heels
How your hips couldn't help but sway and swish
How the smoke curled in and out of your eyes.
I have wanted
Letters from that lover
In our water-puckered hands
Just reading and remembering.
Not make- believe.
Knowing we tell what ought to be truth.

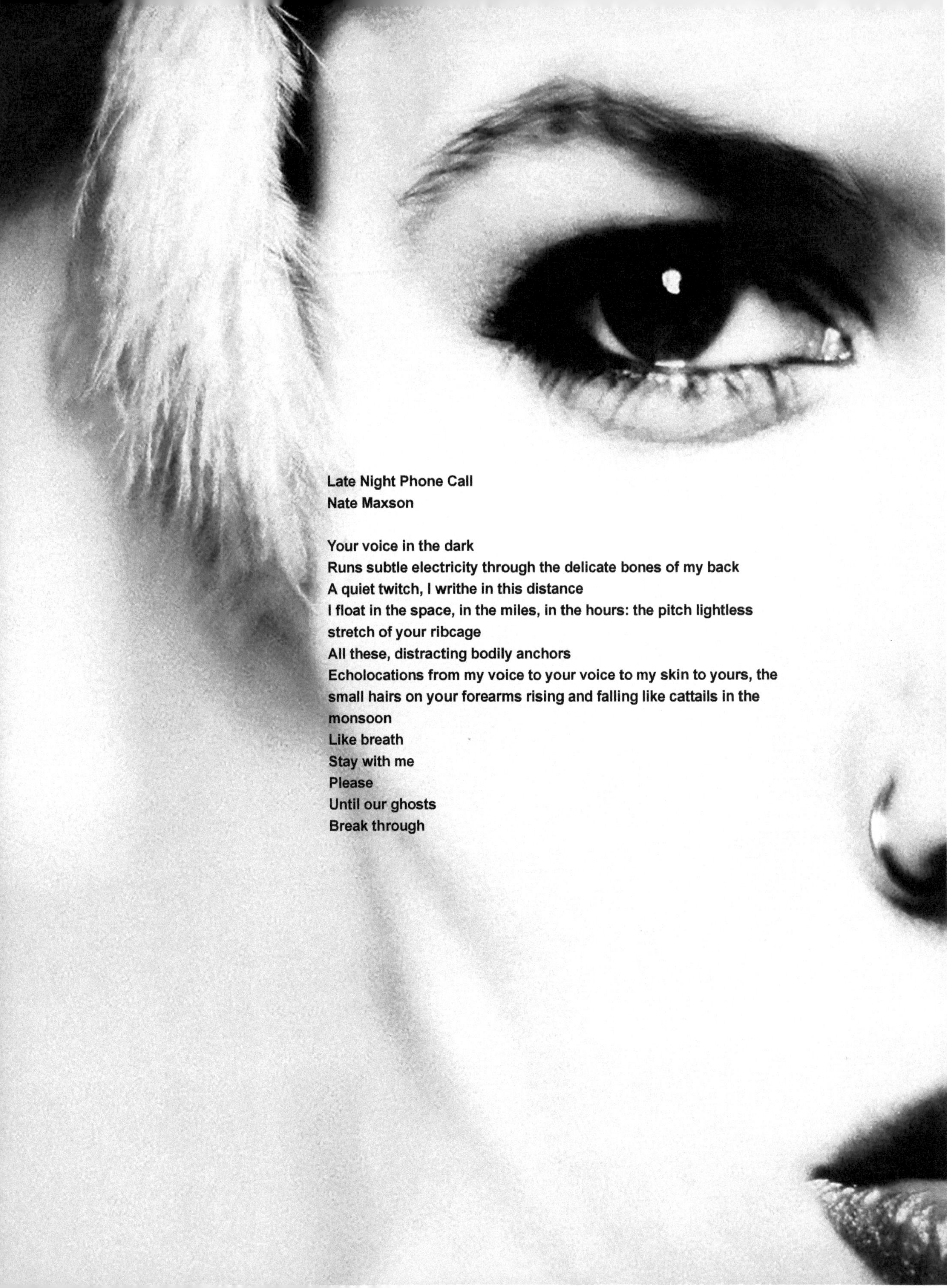

Late Night Phone Call
Nate Maxson

Your voice in the dark
Runs subtle electricity through the delicate bones of my back
A quiet twitch, I writhe in this distance
I float in the space, in the miles, in the hours: the pitch lightless
stretch of your ribcage
All these, distracting bodily anchors
Echolocations from my voice to your voice to my skin to yours, the
small hairs on your forearms rising and falling like cattails in the
monsoon
Like breath
Stay with me
Please
Until our ghosts
Break through

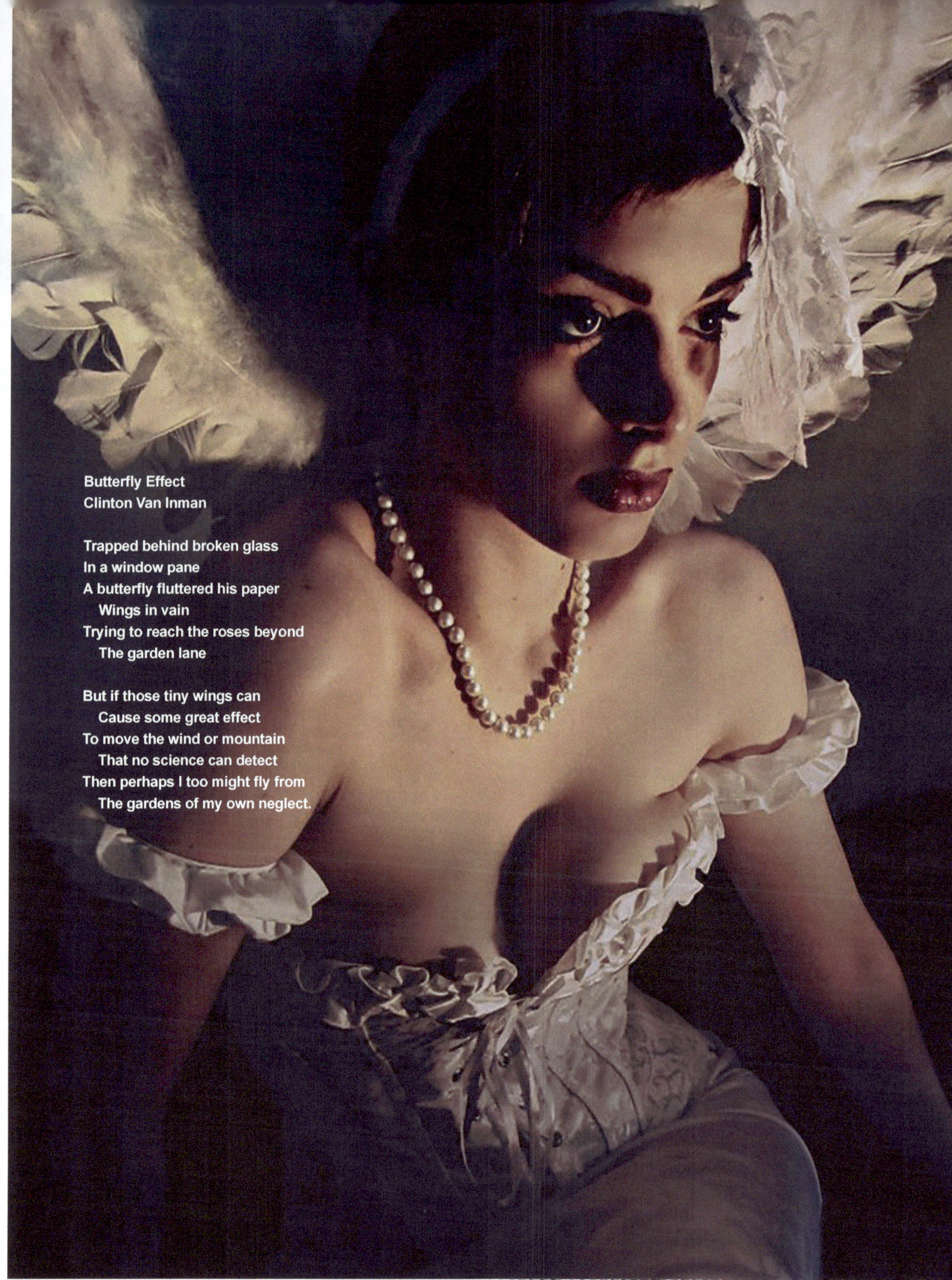

Butterfly Effect
Clinton Van Inman

Trapped behind broken glass
In a window pane
A butterfly fluttered his paper
    Wings in vain
Trying to reach the roses beyond
    The garden lane

But if those tiny wings can
    Cause some great effect
To move the wind or mountain
    That no science can detect
Then perhaps I too might fly from
    The gardens of my own neglect.

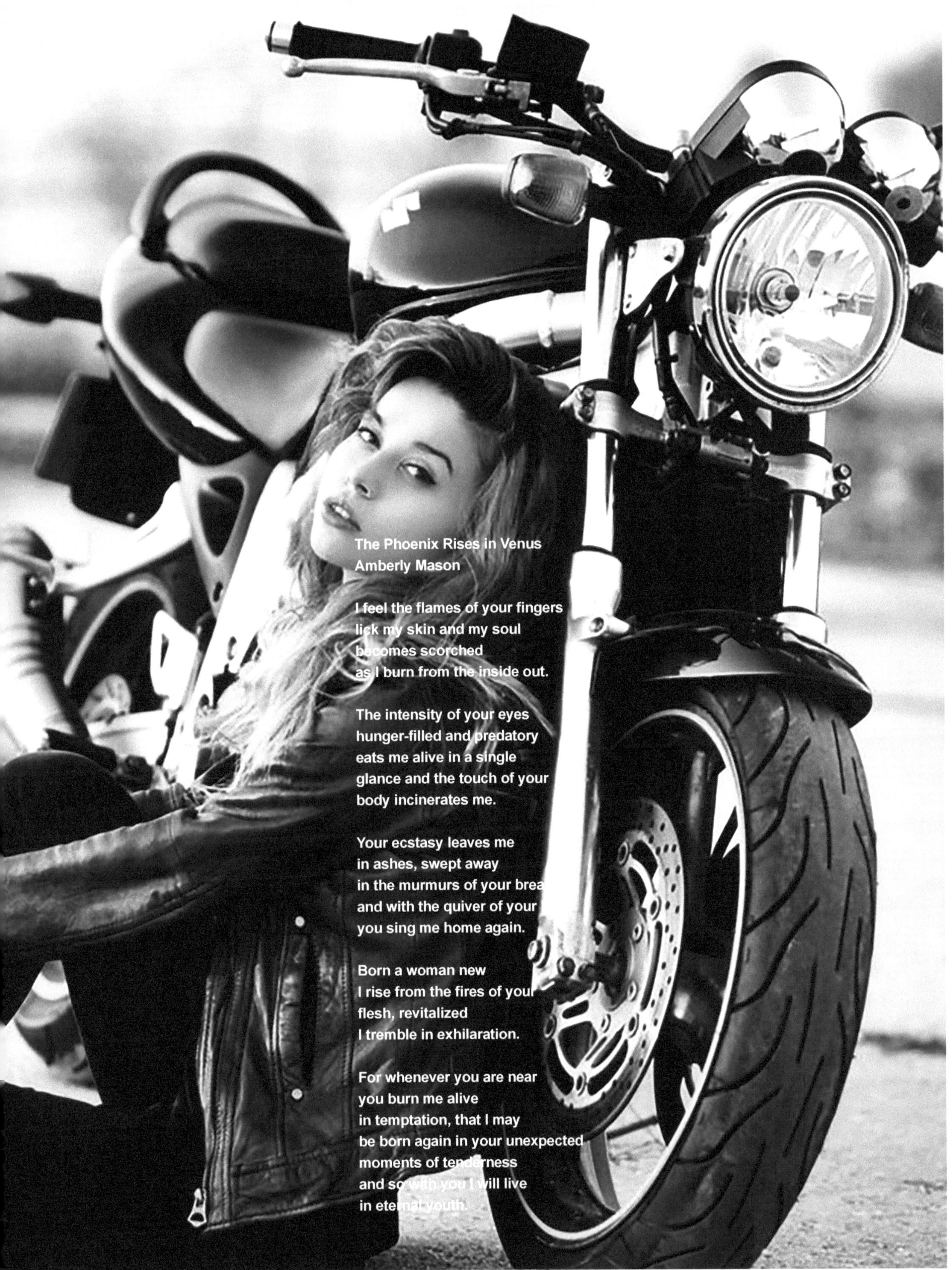

The Phoenix Rises in Venus
Amberly Mason

I feel the flames of your fingers
lick my skin and my soul
becomes scorched
as I burn from the inside out.

The intensity of your eyes
hunger-filled and predatory
eats me alive in a single
glance and the touch of your
body incinerates me.

Your ecstasy leaves me
in ashes, swept away
in the murmurs of your brea
and with the quiver of your
you sing me home again.

Born a woman new
I rise from the fires of you
flesh, revitalized
I tremble in exhilaration.

For whenever you are near
you burn me alive
in temptation, that I may
be born again in your unexpected
moments of tenderness
and so with you I will live
in eternal youth.

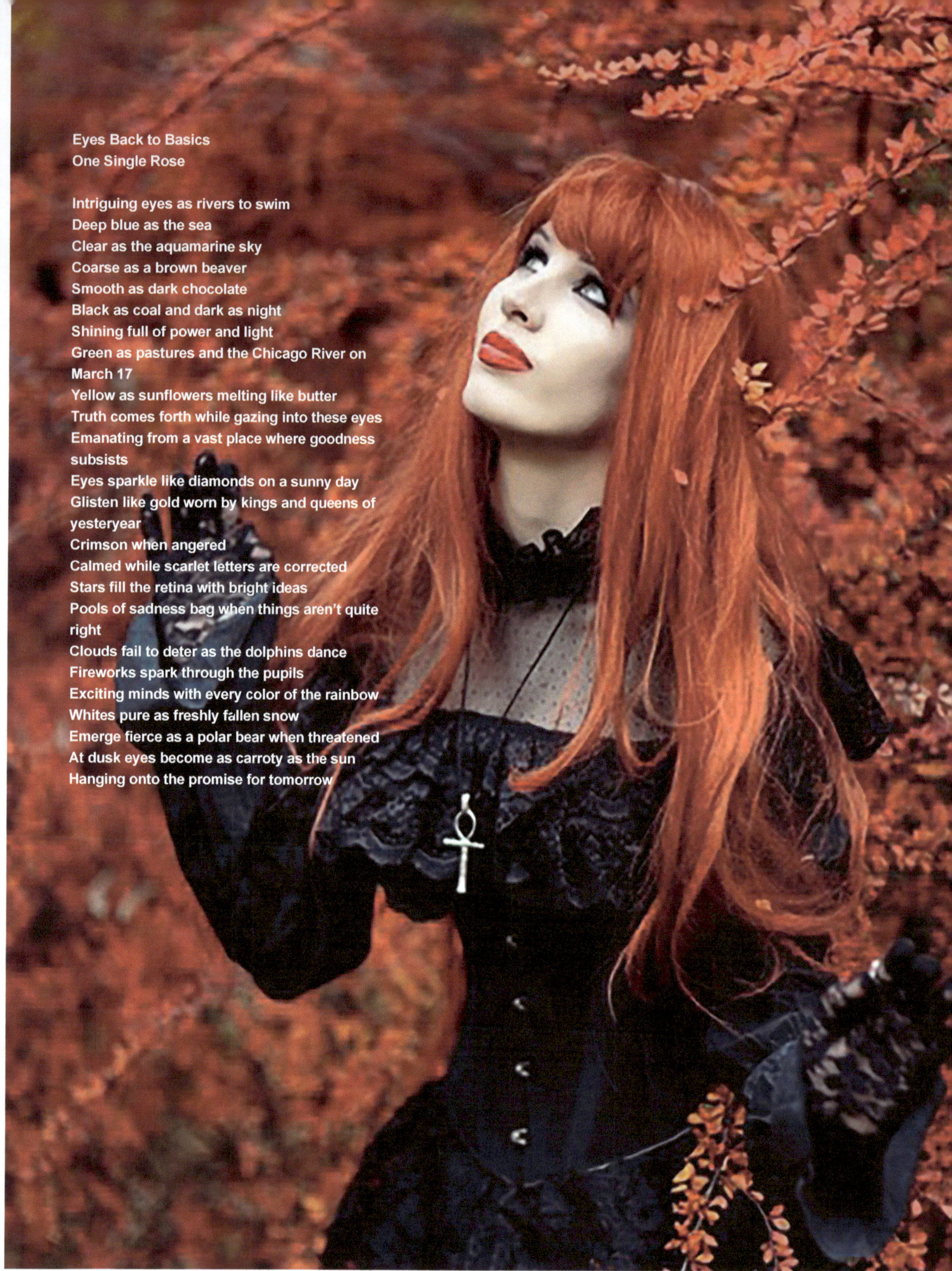

Eyes Back to Basics
One Single Rose

Intriguing eyes as rivers to swim
Deep blue as the sea
Clear as the aquamarine sky
Coarse as a brown beaver
Smooth as dark chocolate
Black as coal and dark as night
Shining full of power and light
Green as pastures and the Chicago River on
March 17
Yellow as sunflowers melting like butter
Truth comes forth while gazing into these eyes
Emanating from a vast place where goodness
subsists
Eyes sparkle like diamonds on a sunny day
Glisten like gold worn by kings and queens of
yesteryear
Crimson when angered
Calmed while scarlet letters are corrected
Stars fill the retina with bright ideas
Pools of sadness bag when things aren't quite
right
Clouds fail to deter as the dolphins dance
Fireworks spark through the pupils
Exciting minds with every color of the rainbow
Whites pure as freshly fallen snow
Emerge fierce as a polar bear when threatened
At dusk eyes become as carroty as the sun
Hanging onto the promise for tomorrow

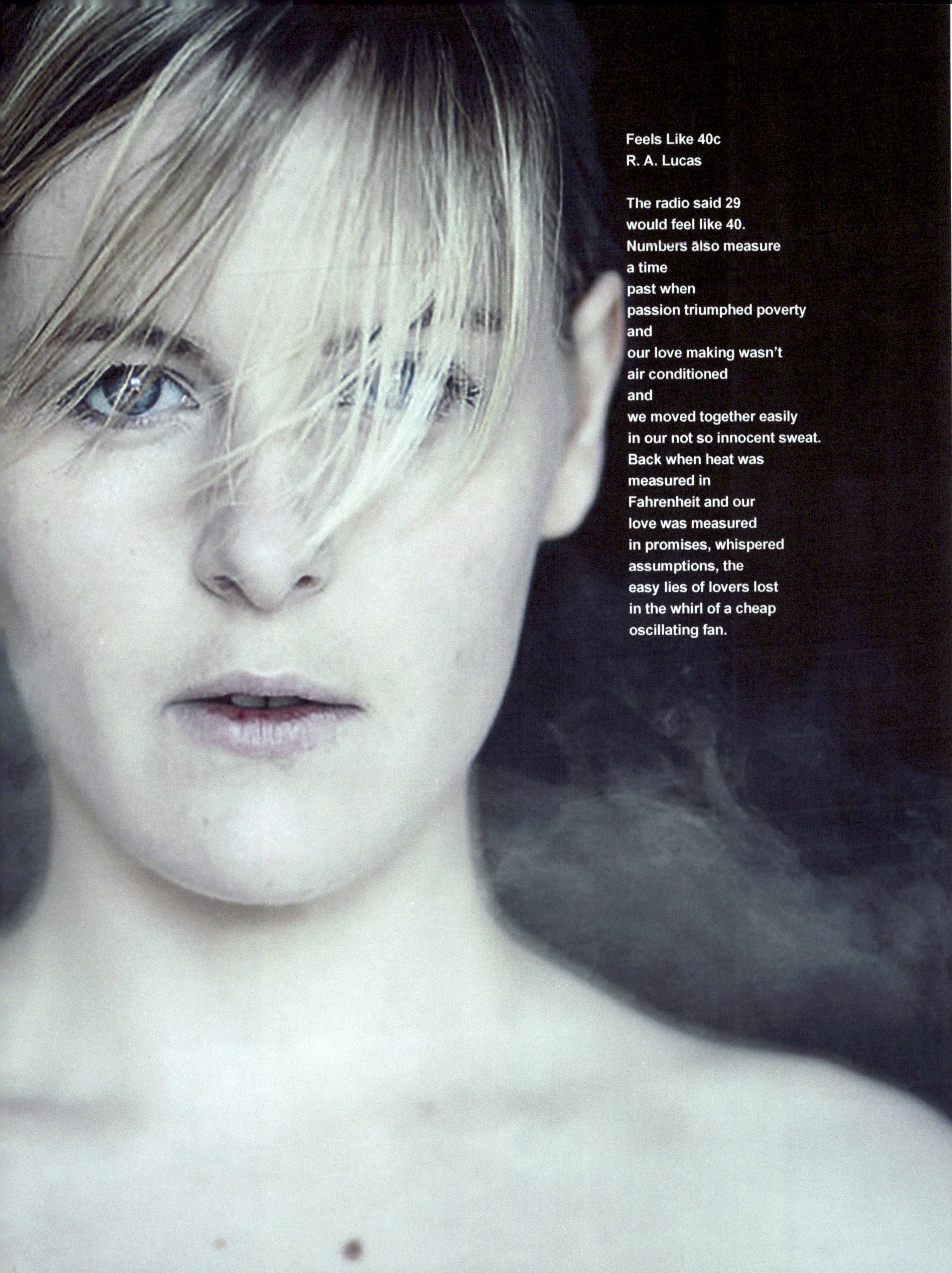

Feels Like 40c
R. A. Lucas

The radio said 29
would feel like 40.
Numbers also measure
a time
past when
passion triumphed poverty
and
our love making wasn't
air conditioned
and
we moved together easily
in our not so innocent sweat.
Back when heat was
measured in
Fahrenheit and our
love was measured
in promises, whispered
assumptions, the
easy lies of lovers lost
in the whirl of a cheap
oscillating fan.

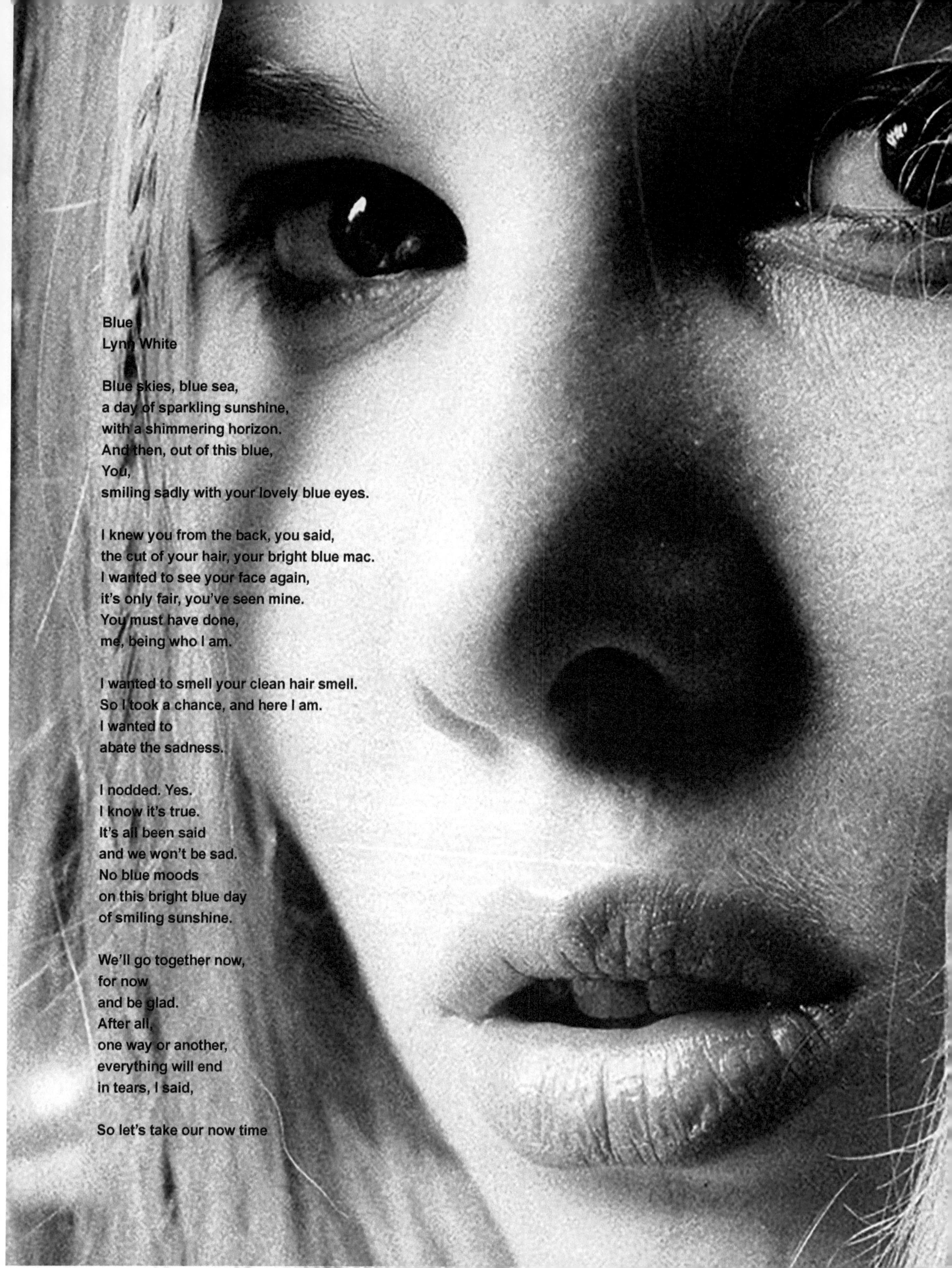
Blue
Lynn White

Blue skies, blue sea,
a day of sparkling sunshine,
with a shimmering horizon.
And then, out of this blue,
You,
smiling sadly with your lovely blue eyes.

I knew you from the back, you said,
the cut of your hair, your bright blue mac.
I wanted to see your face again,
it's only fair, you've seen mine.
You must have done,
me, being who I am.

I wanted to smell your clean hair smell.
So I took a chance, and here I am.
I wanted to
abate the sadness.

I nodded. Yes.
I know it's true.
It's all been said
and we won't be sad.
No blue moods
on this bright blue day
of smiling sunshine.

We'll go together now,
for now
and be glad.
After all,
one way or another,
everything will end
in tears, I said,

So let's take our now time

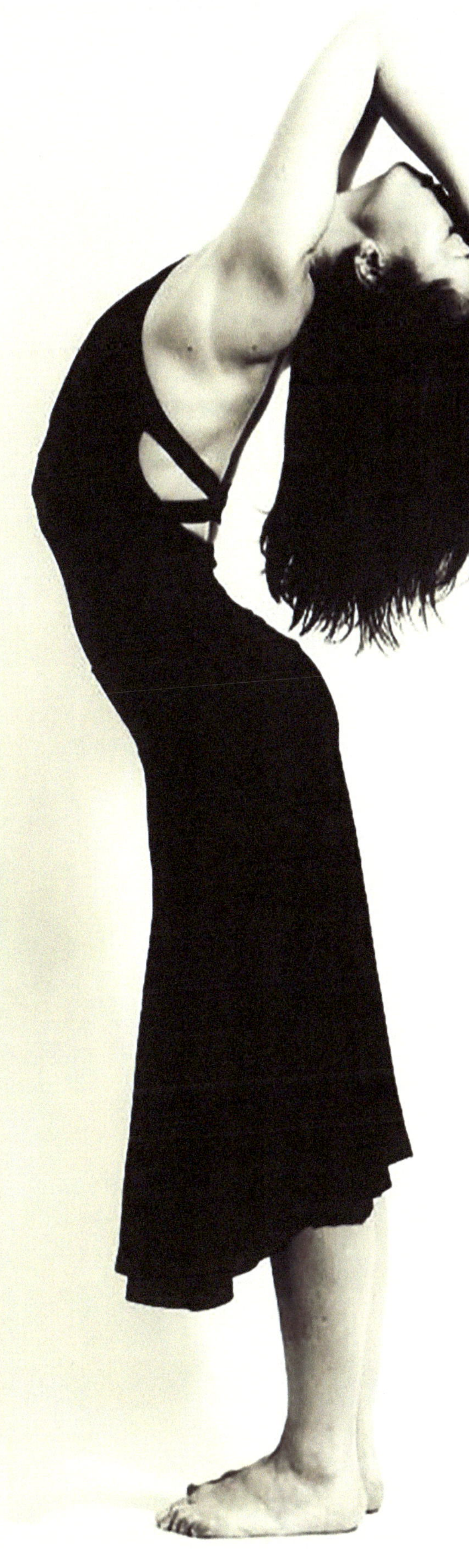

cithara song, strummed lightly as the sun leaps the horizon
William F. DeVault

the dream came again last night. silence begging sound
like hunger or thirst begs ambrosia in cup or bowl or mug.
and music swam in like a barefoot Mexican dancer, bound
to the light like the smoke of fires faded as shadows hug
the corners of the stonework spires that pierce the skies
with hard intentions to a softened grace, placed aloft
on legs of granite and marble and brick. the echo dies
and I am left to ponder another feline dancing, soft
and silent. a smile of curious wonder woven in jaws
that already hold me in their web of kiss and word,
culled from the senses sent soaring by your lavender claws
as they approach, the cool stone by warm feet obscured.
and, as always, you charm the night like an eager lover
to your bidding, your laugh catching on the stars that hover.

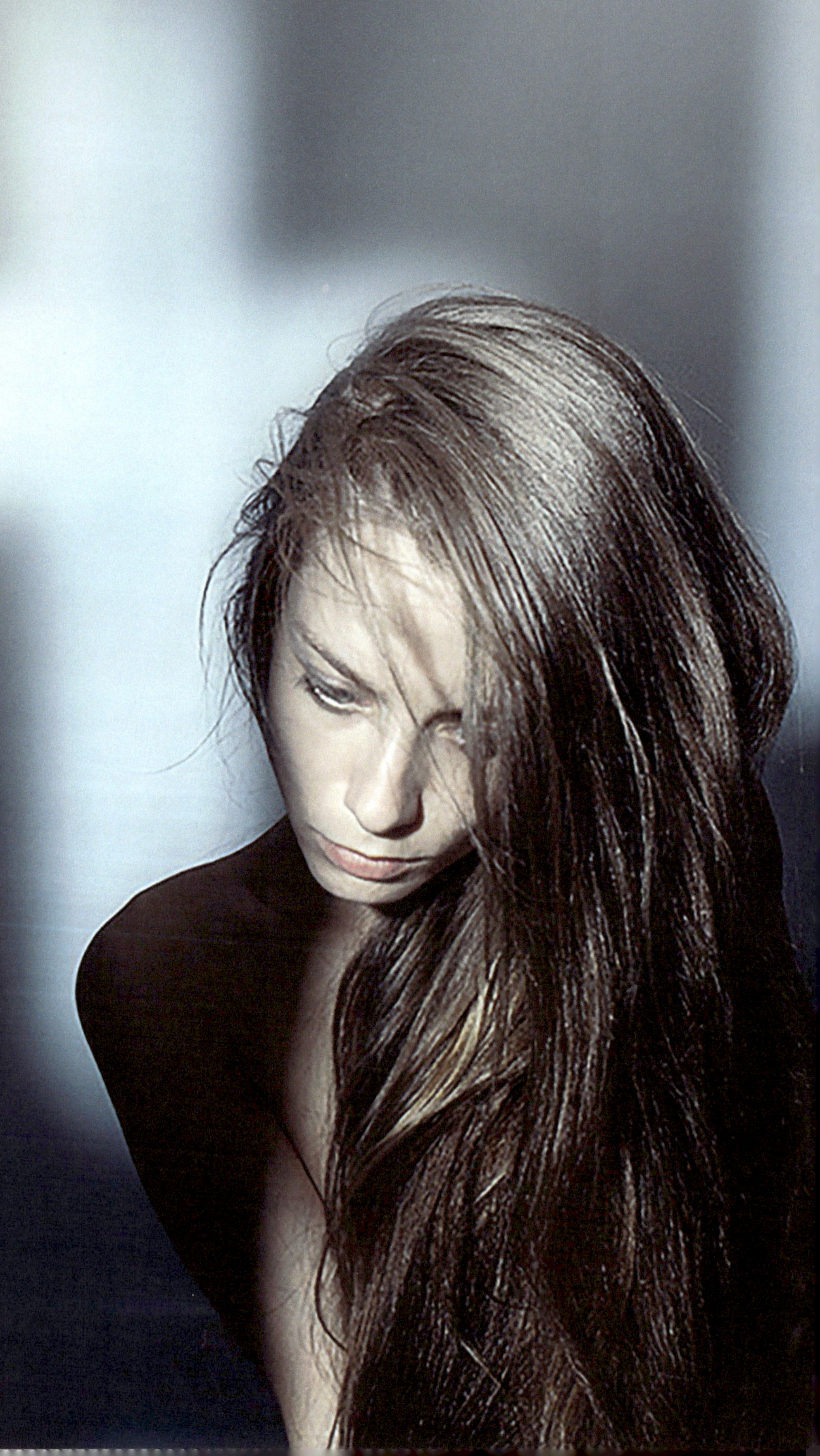

The Fabric Of Creation
Mike Essiq

Lovers weave
the fabric
of creation.
Entering you,
I return to Paradise.
When your flesh
surrounds me,
the Garden
is restored.
Together
we become
much more
than each other -
one tapestry
woven
of two threads.
How many
existences
to arrive
at this life?
The particles dance,
rearrange, renew;
a universe
constantly reborn.
All of this
endless majesty
that my head
might find
the pillow
of your belly,
that my ears
might feel
the beating
of your heart.
Every breath,
divine
and precious;
each moment
a new world.

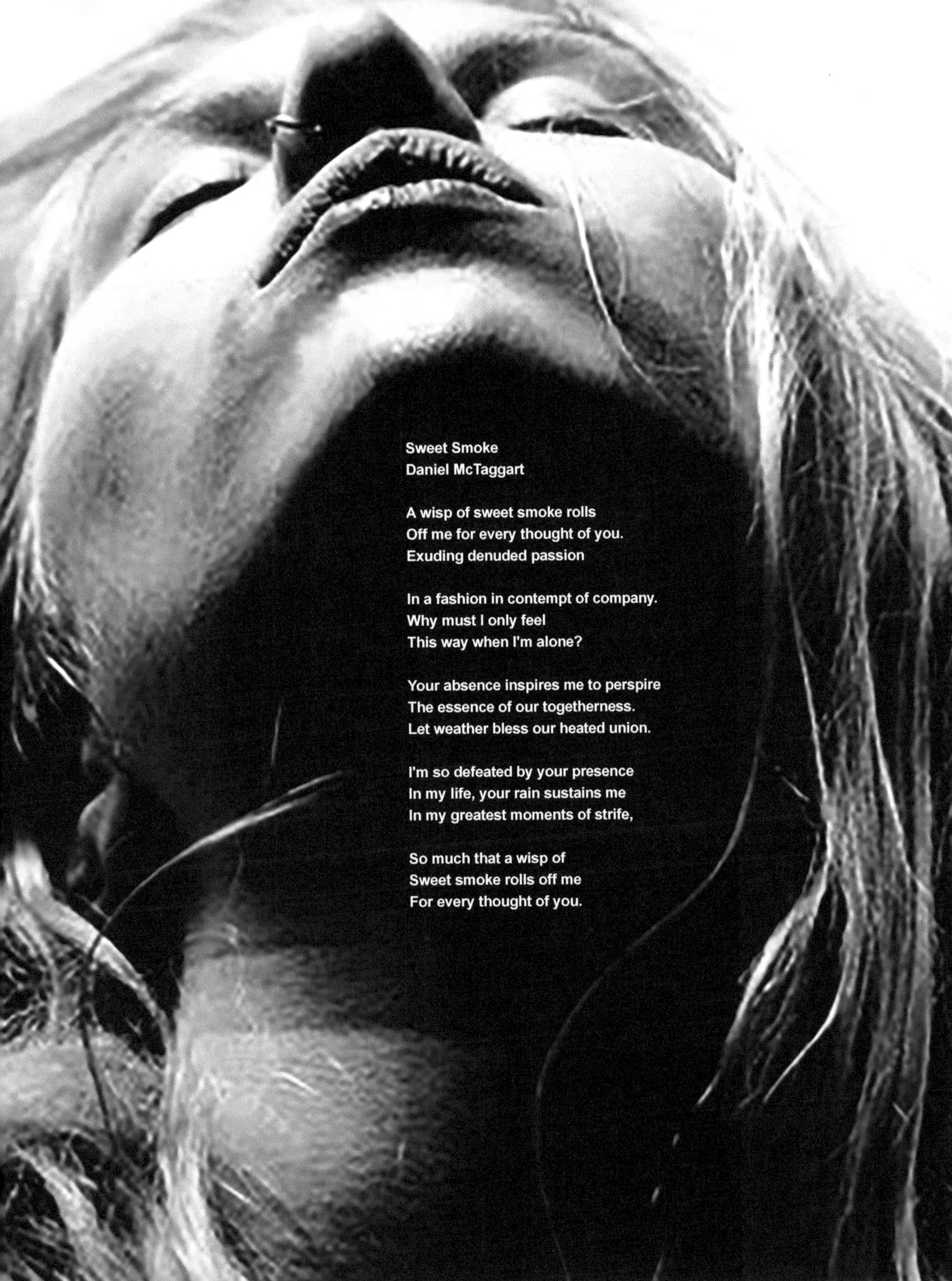

Sweet Smoke
Daniel McTaggart

A wisp of sweet smoke rolls
Off me for every thought of you.
Exuding denuded passion

In a fashion in contempt of company.
Why must I only feel
This way when I'm alone?

Your absence inspires me to perspire
The essence of our togetherness.
Let weather bless our heated union.

I'm so defeated by your presence
In my life, your rain sustains me
In my greatest moments of strife,

So much that a wisp of
Sweet smoke rolls off me
For every thought of you.

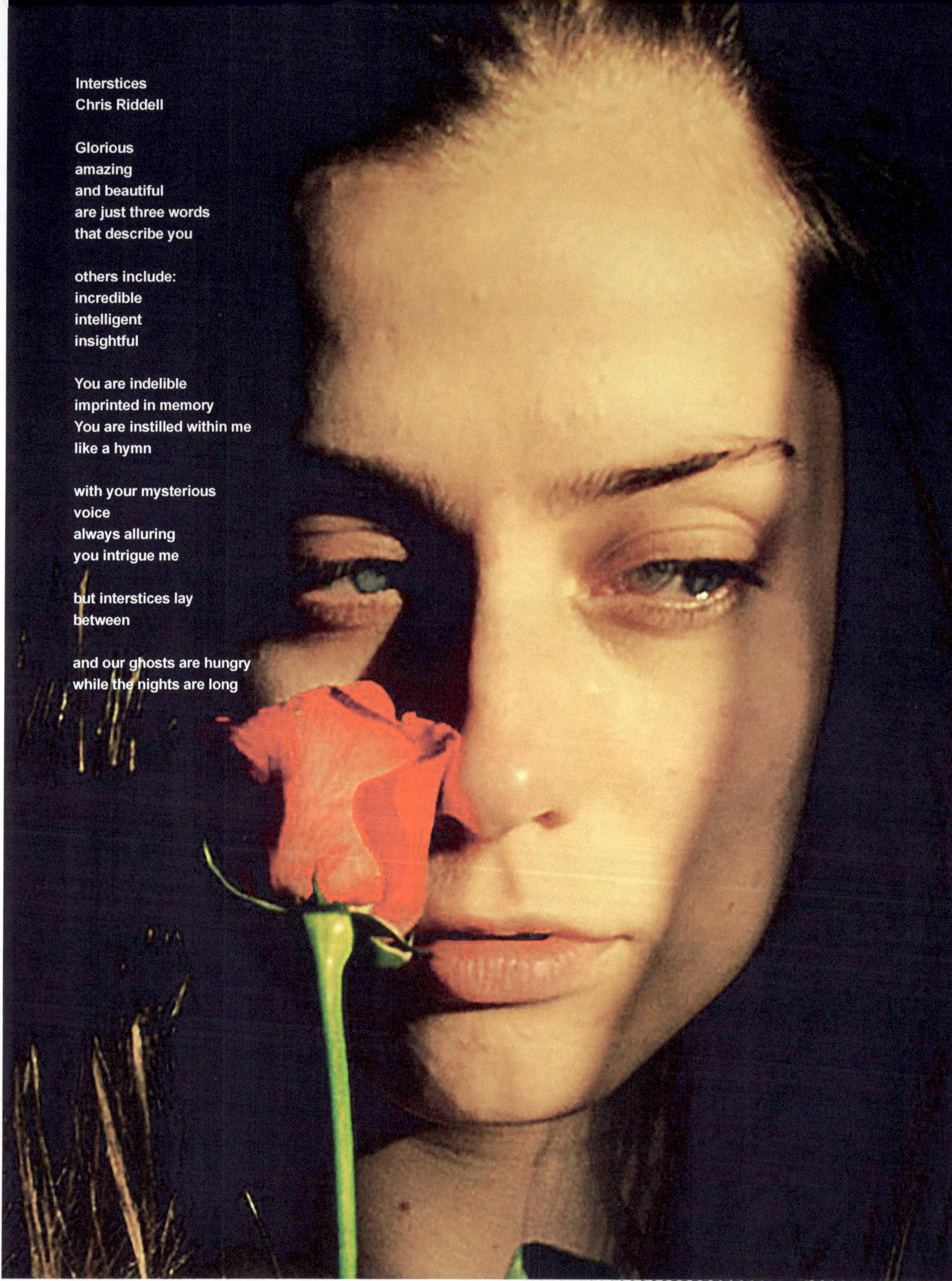

Interstices
Chris Riddell

Glorious
amazing
and beautiful
are just three words
that describe you

others include:
incredible
intelligent
insightful

You are indelible
imprinted in memory
You are instilled within me
like a hymn

with your mysterious
voice
always alluring
you intrigue me

but interstices lay
between

and our ghosts are hungry
while the nights are long

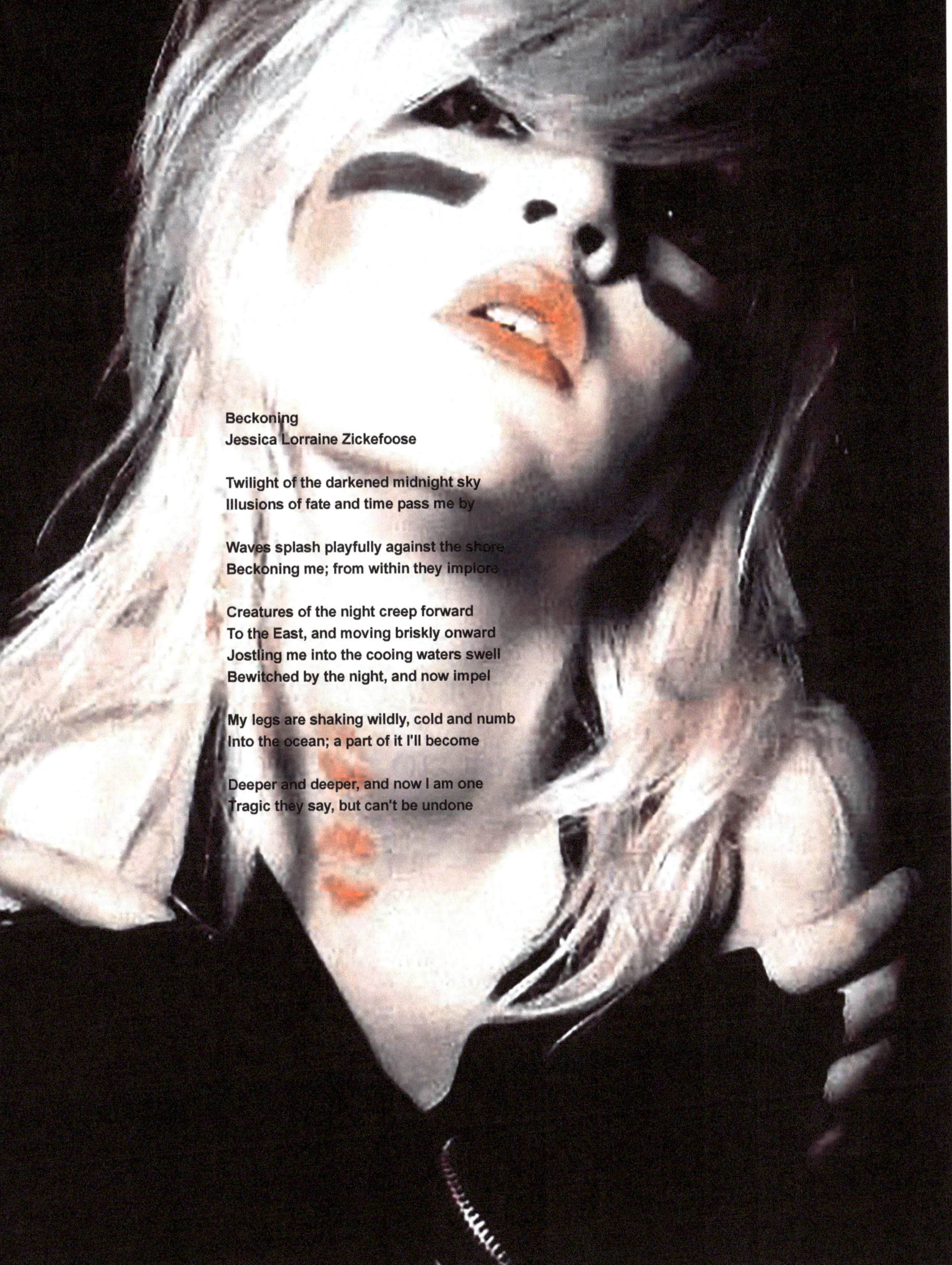

Beckoning
Jessica Lorraine Zickefoose

Twilight of the darkened midnight sky
Illusions of fate and time pass me by

Waves splash playfully against the shore
Beckoning me; from within they implore

Creatures of the night creep forward
To the East, and moving briskly onward
Jostling me into the cooing waters swell
Bewitched by the night, and now impel

My legs are shaking wildly, cold and numb
Into the ocean; a part of it I'll become

Deeper and deeper, and now I am one
Tragic they say, but can't be undone

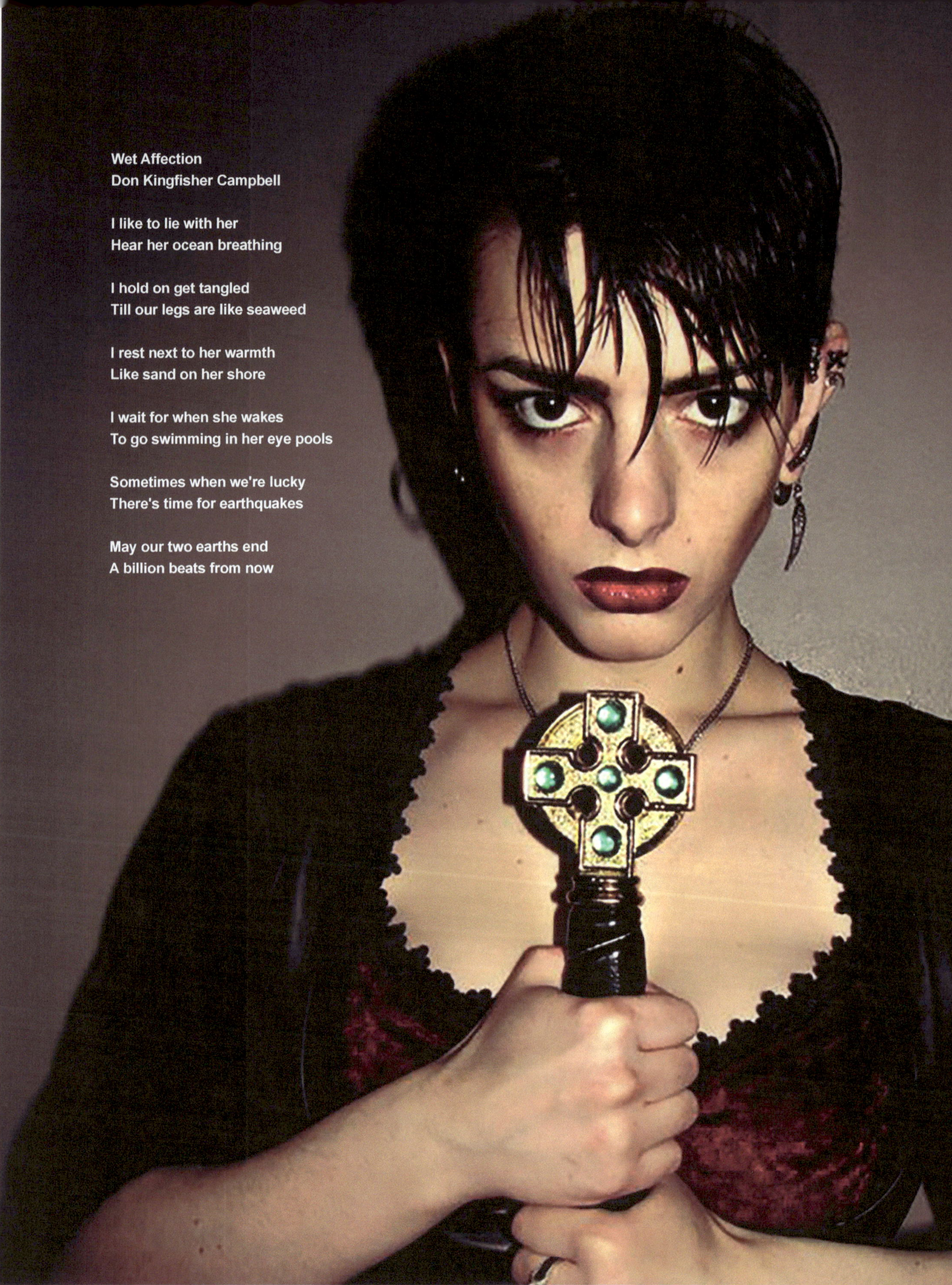

Wet Affection
Don Kingfisher Campbell

I like to lie with her
Hear her ocean breathing

I hold on get tangled
Till our legs are like seaweed

I rest next to her warmth
Like sand on her shore

I wait for when she wakes
To go swimming in her eye pools

Sometimes when we're lucky
There's time for earthquakes

May our two earths end
A billion beats from now

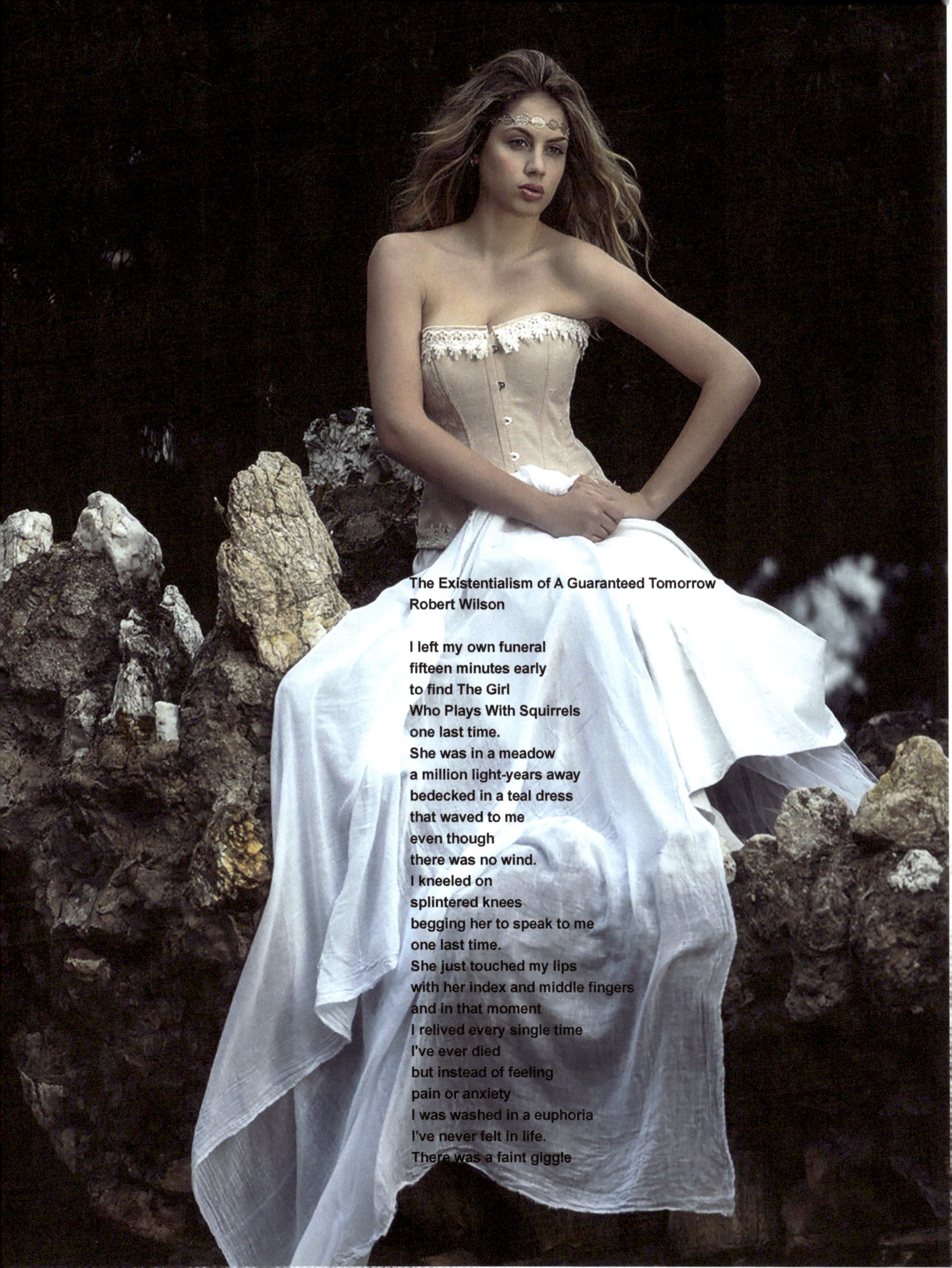

The Existentialism of A Guaranteed Tomorrow
Robert Wilson

I left my own funeral
fifteen minutes early
to find The Girl
Who Plays With Squirrels
one last time.
She was in a meadow
a million light-years away
bedecked in a teal dress
that waved to me
even though
there was no wind.
I kneeled on
splintered knees
begging her to speak to me
one last time.
She just touched my lips
with her index and middle fingers
and in that moment
I relived every single time
I've ever died
but instead of feeling
pain or anxiety
I was washed in a euphoria
I've never felt in life.
There was a faint giggle

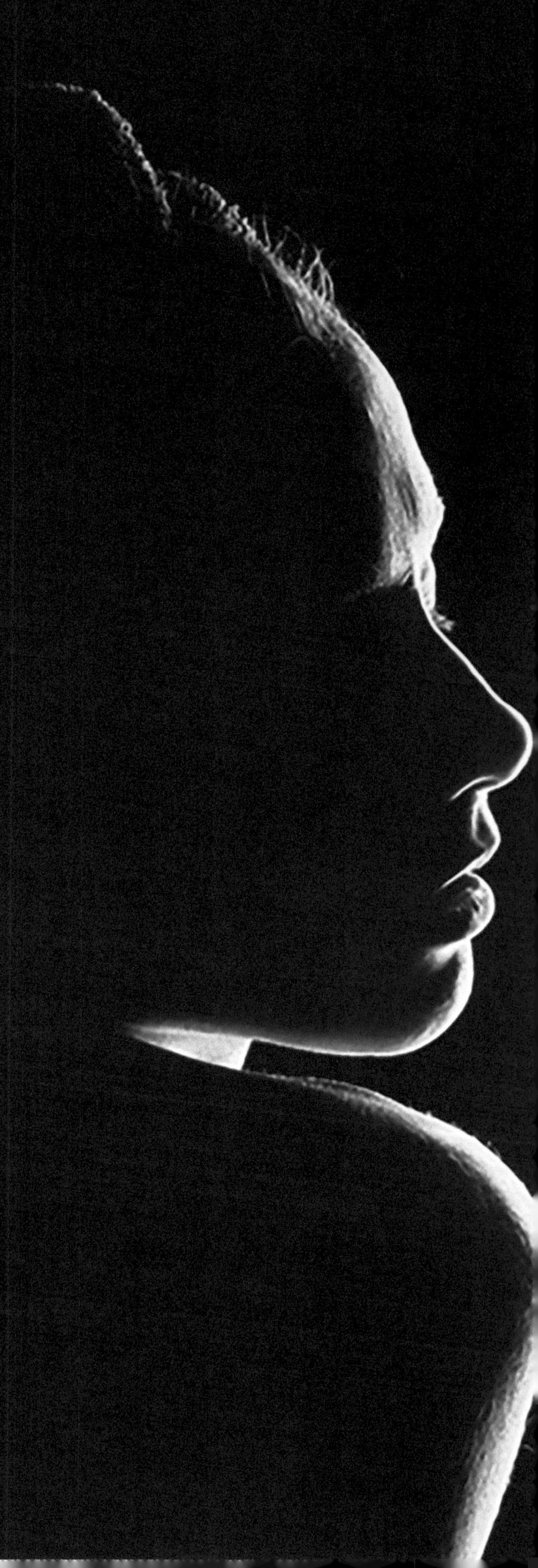

Love is, All is
Strider Marcus Jones

love is,
all islight
and dark,
shade and shadow,
high-low
wide-narrow
crater under rainbow.
tramp or truffle you chance to meet
and take your time to share and eat;
a mythical ark
in-out skylark,
so fluttery butterfly in buddleia stomach
that wakes you up
more muttery in your headwith
jade of jealousy
and truest thread
come concave and convex,
mirrored and mouthed in images and text
with-without key,
but only borrowed
today and tomorrowed
and after that, what will besomething
ethereal
deaths' music can't serial,
alone, then together
in its own weather
sensual and free.

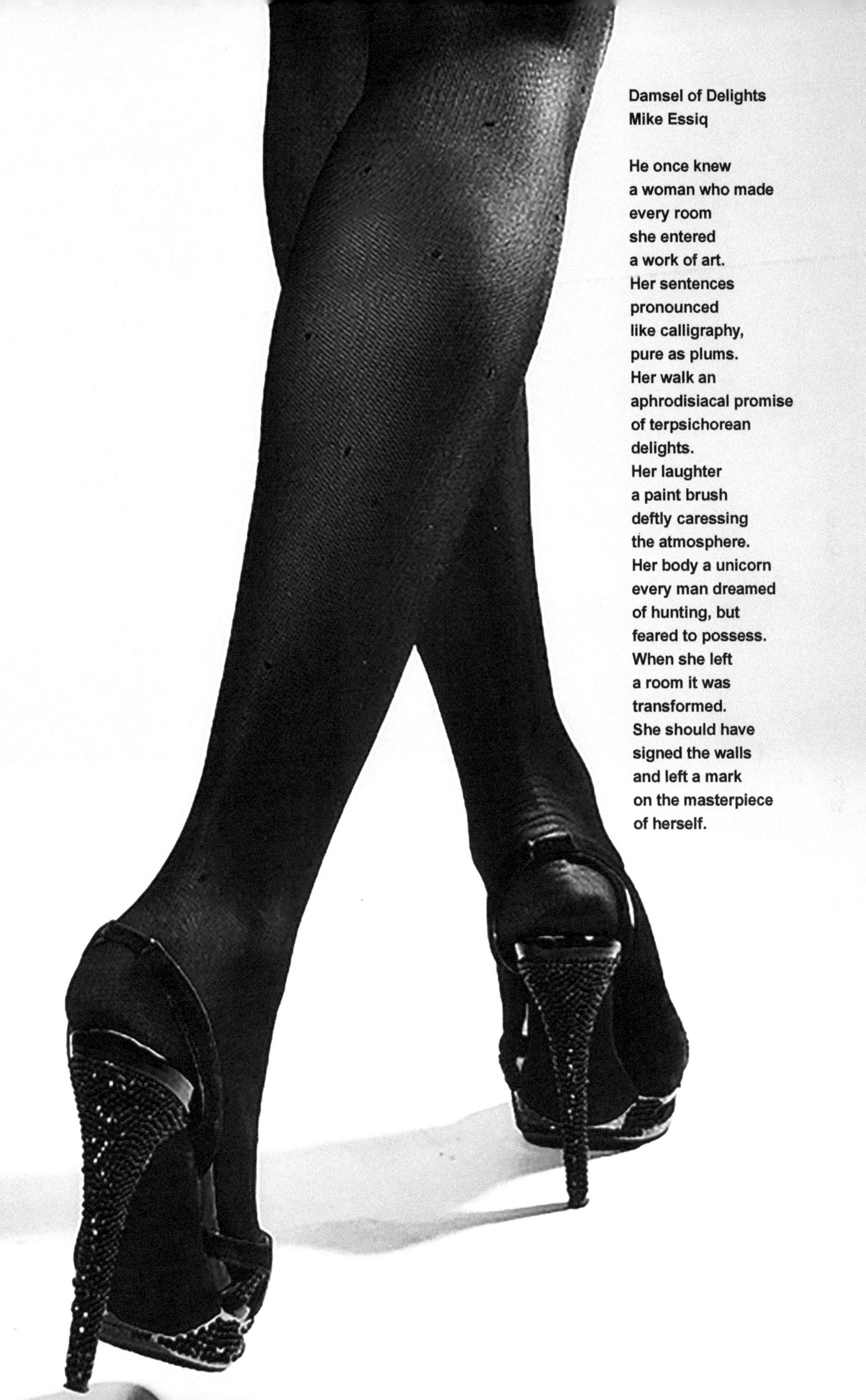
Damsel of Delights
Mike Essiq

He once knew
a woman who made
every room
she entered
a work of art.
Her sentences
pronounced
like calligraphy,
pure as plums.
Her walk an
aphrodisiacal promise
of terpsichorean
delights.
Her laughter
a paint brush
deftly caressing
the atmosphere.
Her body a unicorn
every man dreamed
of hunting, but
feared to possess.
When she left
a room it was
transformed.
She should have
signed the walls
and left a mark
on the masterpiece
of herself.

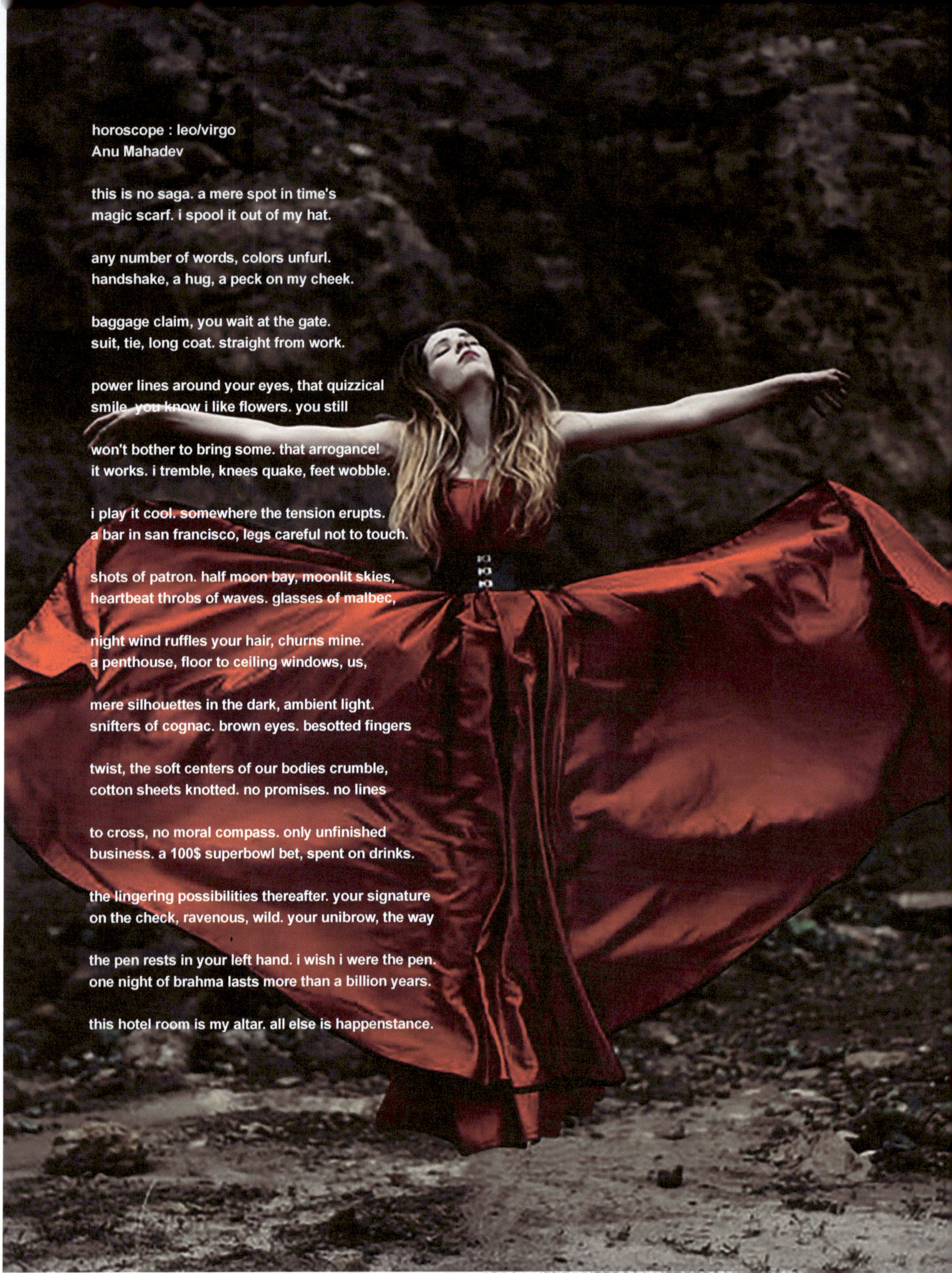

horoscope : leo/virgo
Anu Mahadev

this is no saga. a mere spot in time's
magic scarf. i spool it out of my hat.

any number of words, colors unfurl.
handshake, a hug, a peck on my cheek.

baggage claim, you wait at the gate.
suit, tie, long coat. straight from work.

power lines around your eyes, that quizzical
smile. you know i like flowers. you still

won't bother to bring some. that arrogance!
it works. i tremble, knees quake, feet wobble.

i play it cool. somewhere the tension erupts.
a bar in san francisco, legs careful not to touch.

shots of patron. half moon bay, moonlit skies,
heartbeat throbs of waves. glasses of malbec,

night wind ruffles your hair, churns mine.
a penthouse, floor to ceiling windows, us,

mere silhouettes in the dark, ambient light.
snifters of cognac. brown eyes. besotted fingers

twist, the soft centers of our bodies crumble,
cotton sheets knotted. no promises. no lines

to cross, no moral compass. only unfinished
business. a 100$ superbowl bet, spent on drinks.

the lingering possibilities thereafter. your signature
on the check, ravenous, wild. your unibrow, the way

the pen rests in your left hand. i wish i were the pen.
one night of brahma lasts more than a billion years.

this hotel room is my altar. all else is happenstance.

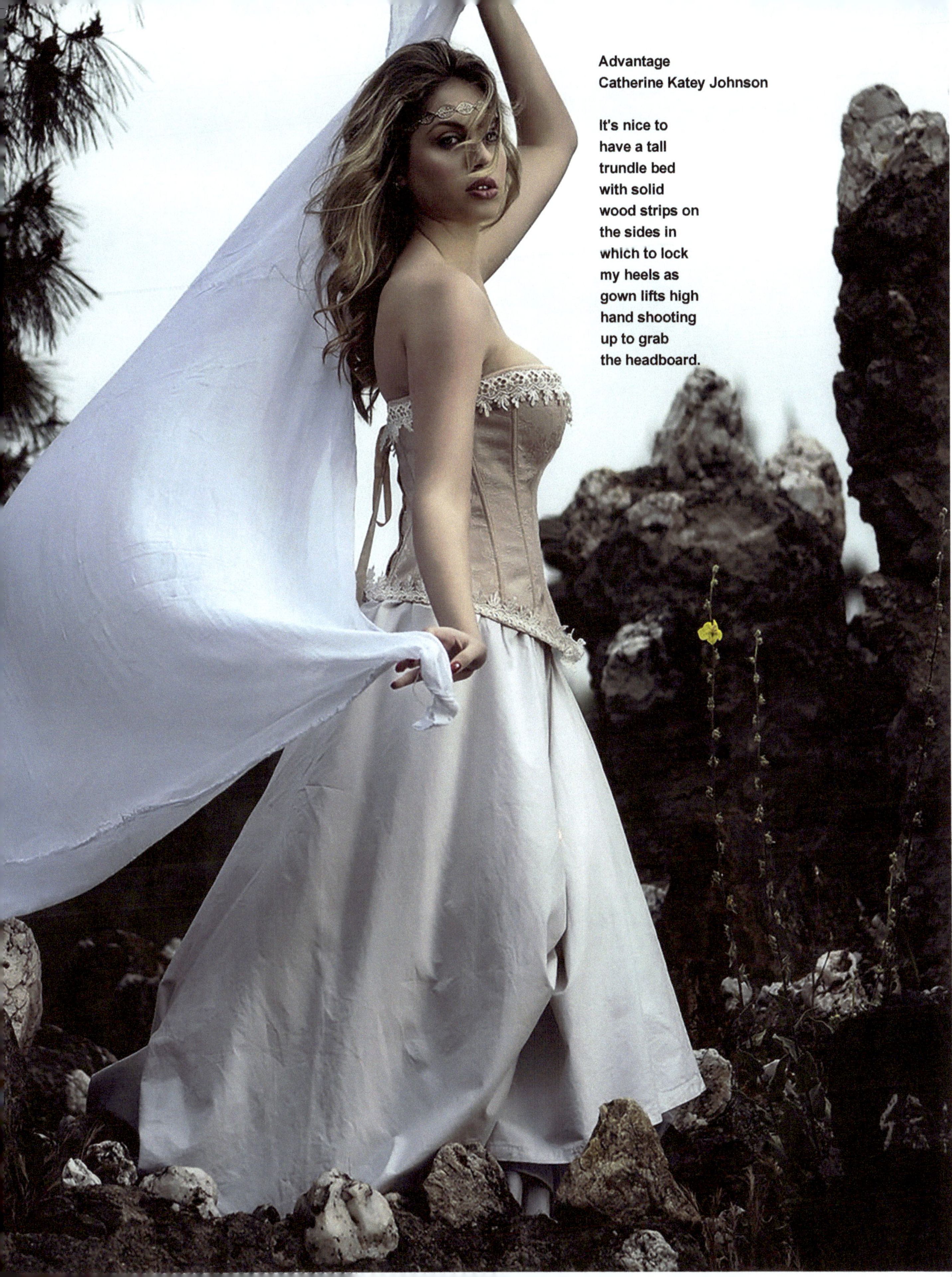

Advantage
Catherine Katey Johnson

It's nice to
have a tall
trundle bed
with solid
wood strips on
the sides in
which to lock
my heels as
gown lifts high
hand shooting
up to grab
the headboard.

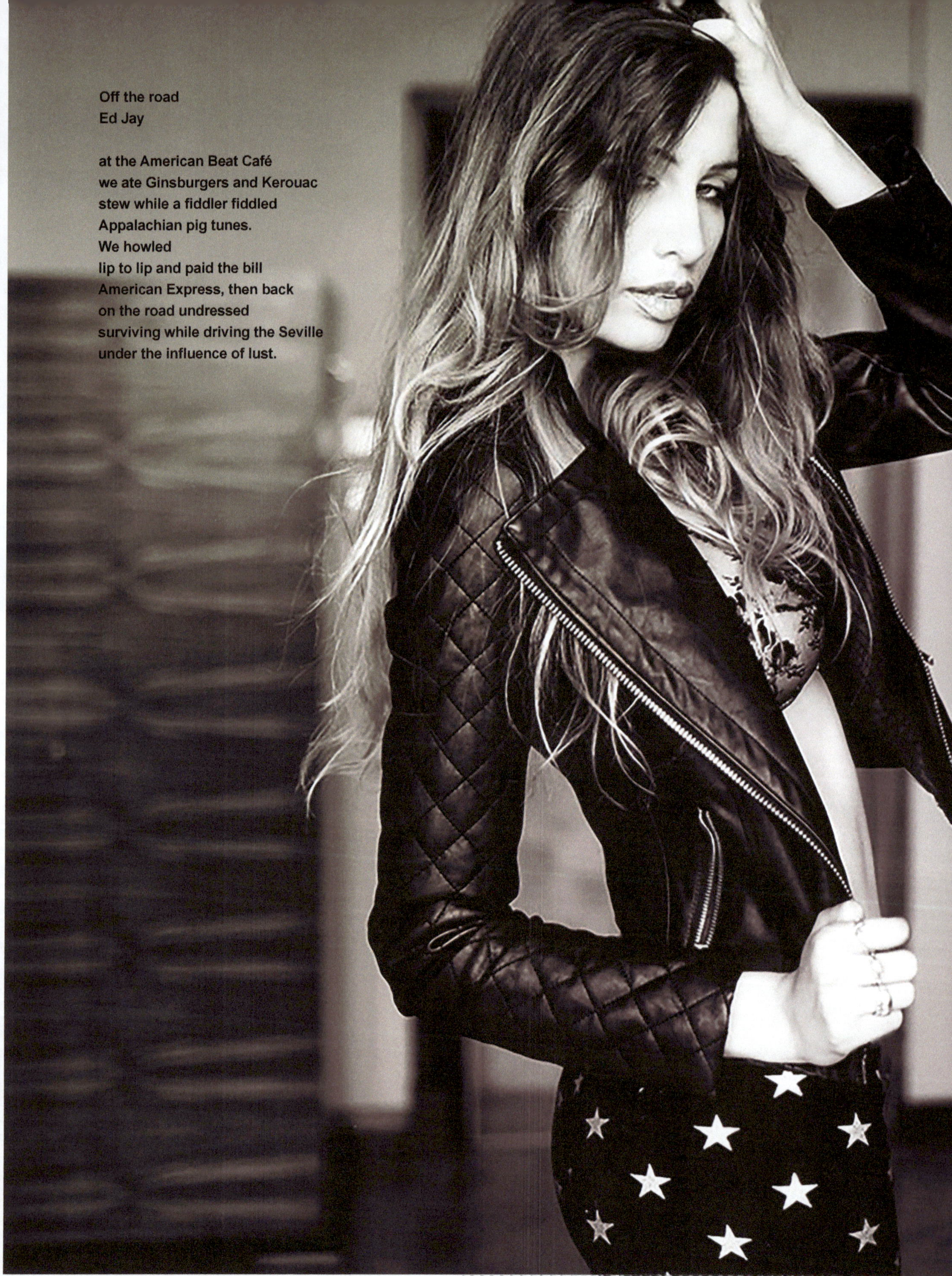

Off the road
Ed Jay

at the American Beat Café
we ate Ginsburgers and Kerouac
stew while a fiddler fiddled
Appalachian pig tunes.
We howled
lip to lip and paid the bill
American Express, then back
on the road undressed
surviving while driving the Seville
under the influence of lust.

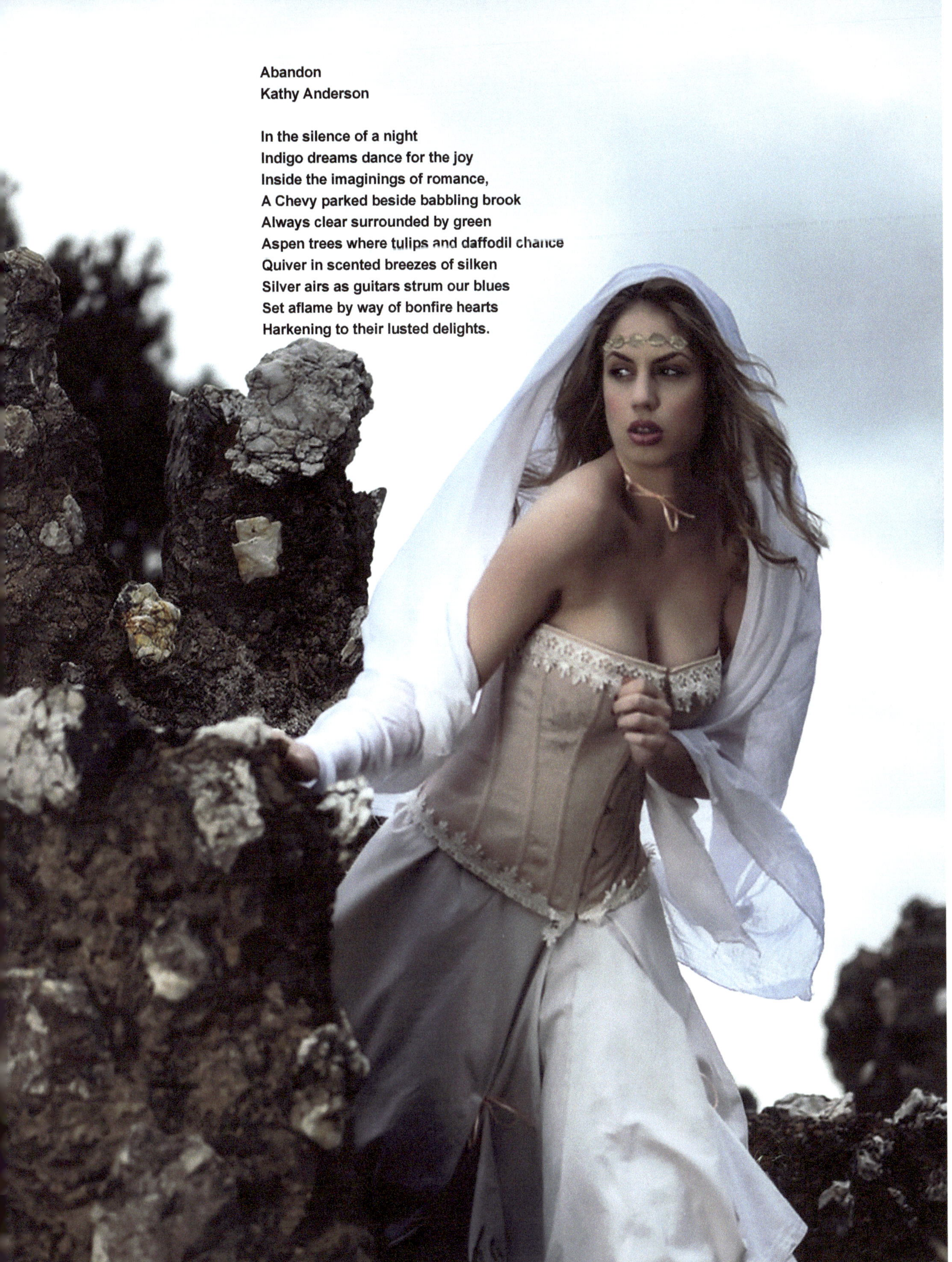

Abandon
Kathy Anderson

In the silence of a night
Indigo dreams dance for the joy
Inside the imaginings of romance,
A Chevy parked beside babbling brook
Always clear surrounded by green
Aspen trees where tulips and daffodil chance
Quiver in scented breezes of silken
Silver airs as guitars strum our blues
Set aflame by way of bonfire hearts
Harkening to their lusted delights.

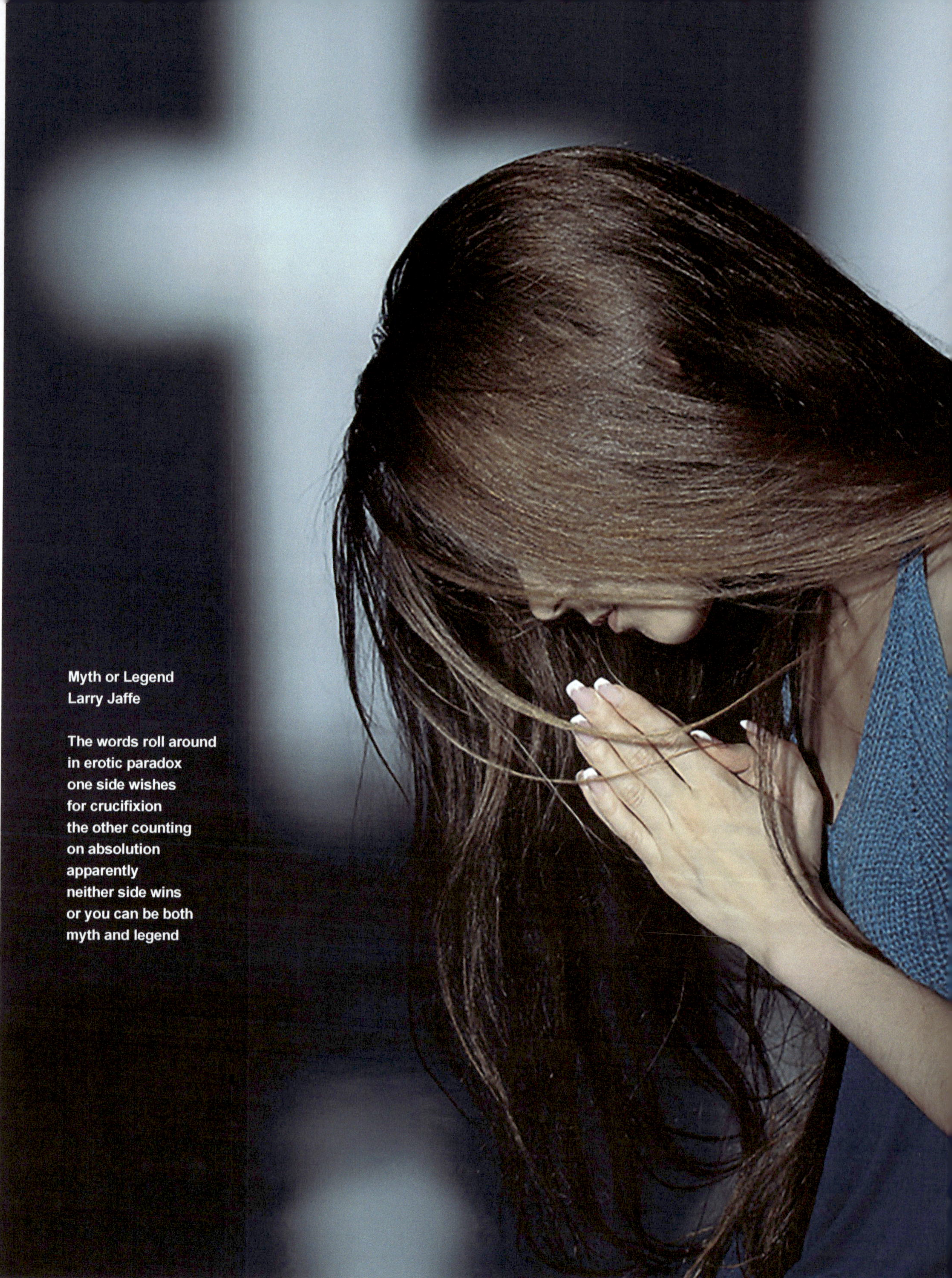

Myth or Legend
Larry Jaffe

The words roll around
in erotic paradox
one side wishes
for crucifixion
the other counting
on absolution
apparently
neither side wins
or you can be both
myth and legend

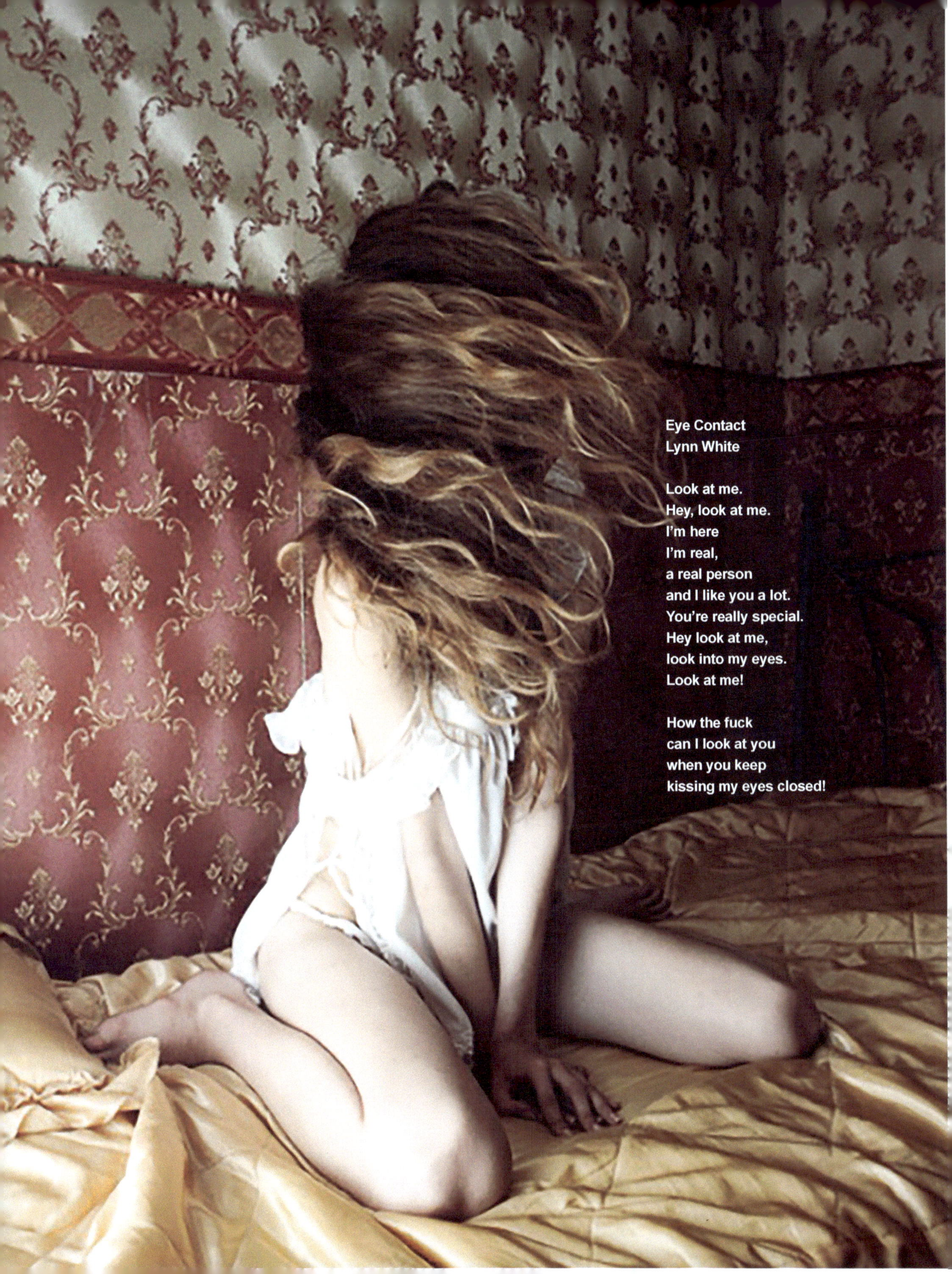

Eye Contact
Lynn White

Look at me.
Hey, look at me.
I'm here
I'm real,
a real person
and I like you a lot.
You're really special.
Hey look at me,
look into my eyes.
Look at me!

How the fuck
can I look at you
when you keep
kissing my eyes closed!

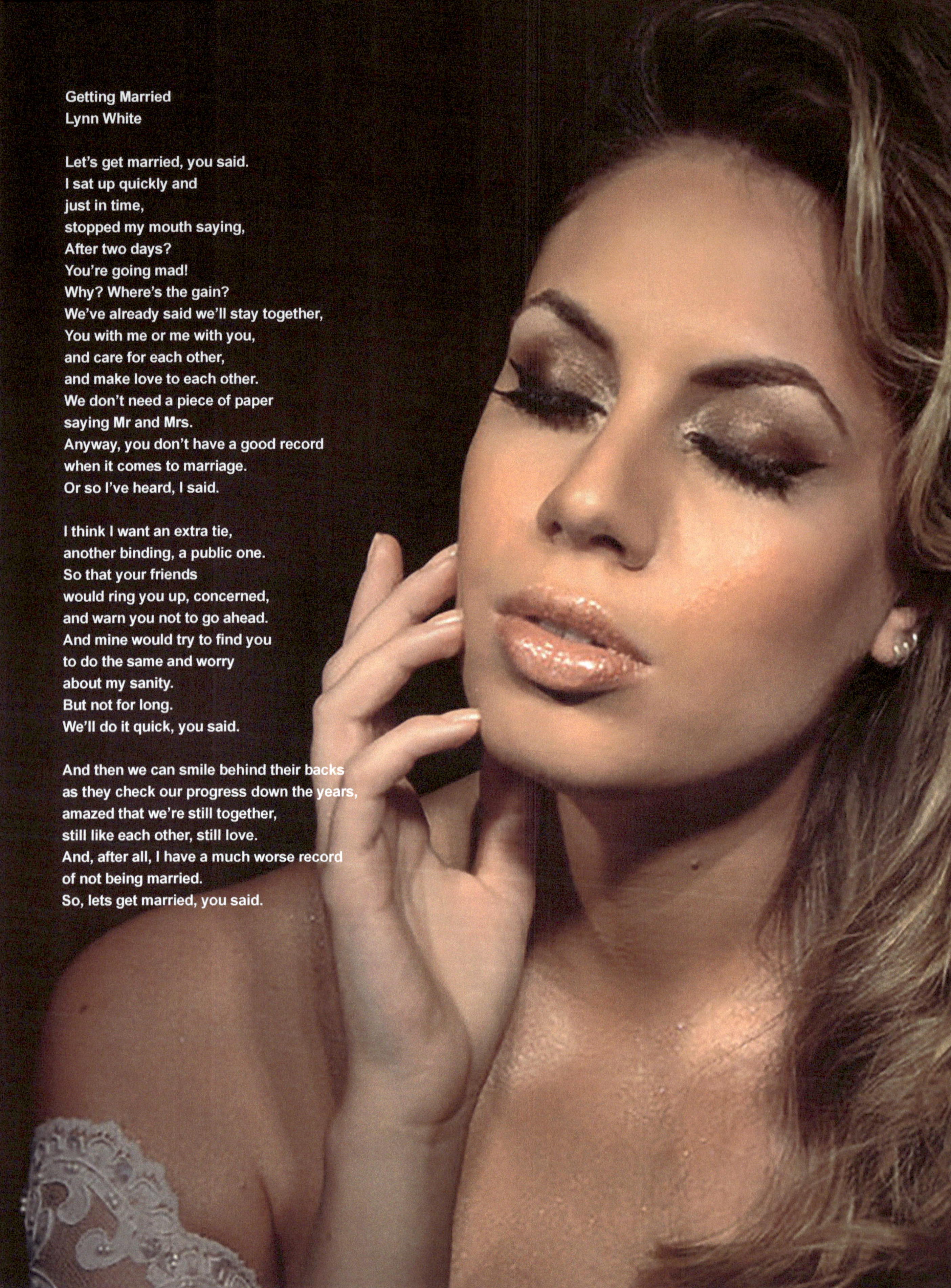
Getting Married
Lynn White

Let's get married, you said.
I sat up quickly and
just in time,
stopped my mouth saying,
After two days?
You're going mad!
Why? Where's the gain?
We've already said we'll stay together,
You with me or me with you,
and care for each other,
and make love to each other.
We don't need a piece of paper
saying Mr and Mrs.
Anyway, you don't have a good record
when it comes to marriage.
Or so I've heard, I said.

I think I want an extra tie,
another binding, a public one.
So that your friends
would ring you up, concerned,
and warn you not to go ahead.
And mine would try to find you
to do the same and worry
about my sanity.
But not for long.
We'll do it quick, you said.

And then we can smile behind their backs
as they check our progress down the years,
amazed that we're still together,
still like each other, still love.
And, after all, I have a much worse record
of not being married.
So, lets get married, you said.

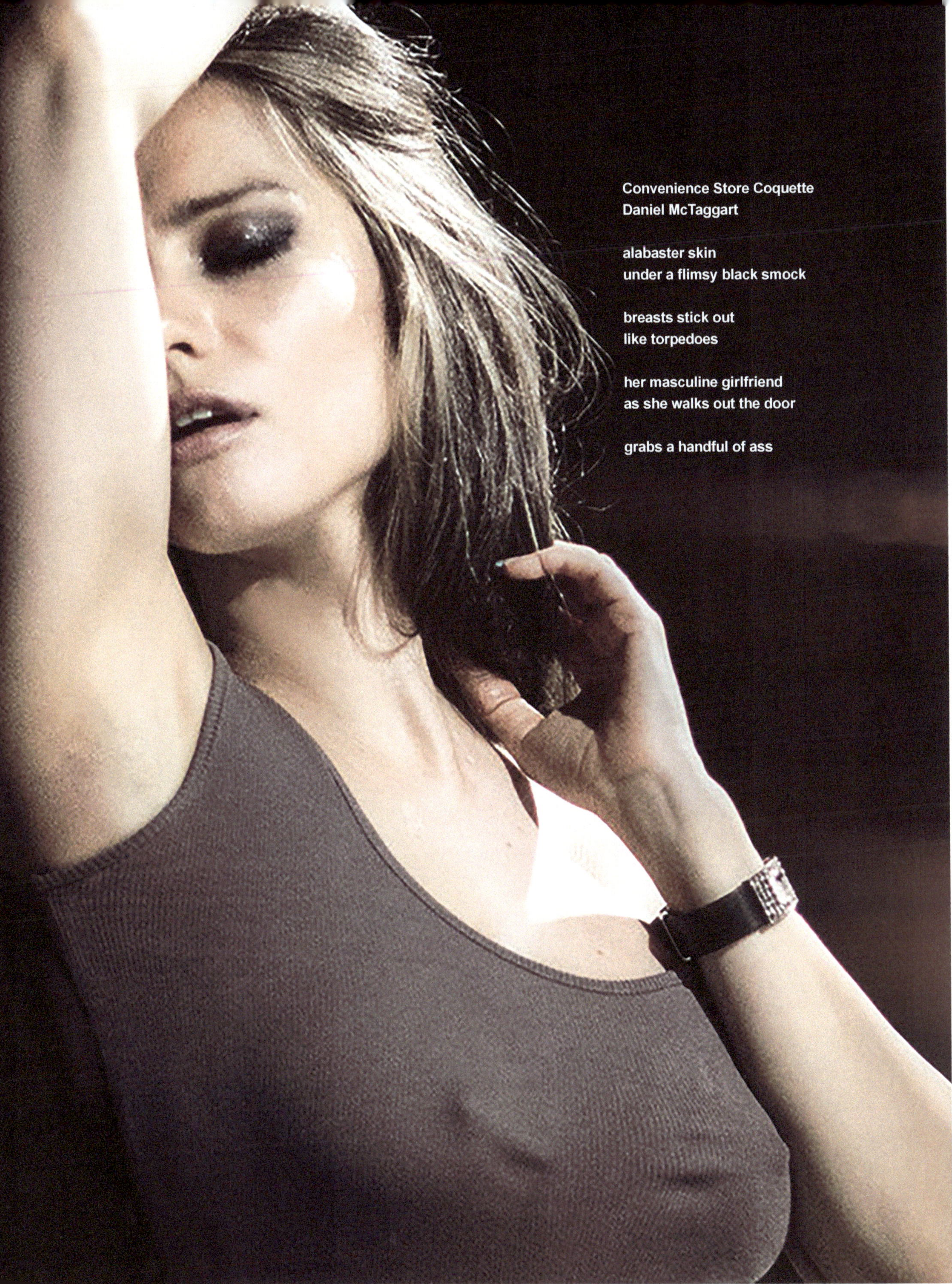

Convenience Store Coquette
Daniel McTaggart

alabaster skin
under a flimsy black smock

breasts stick out
like torpedoes

her masculine girlfriend
as she walks out the door

grabs a handful of ass

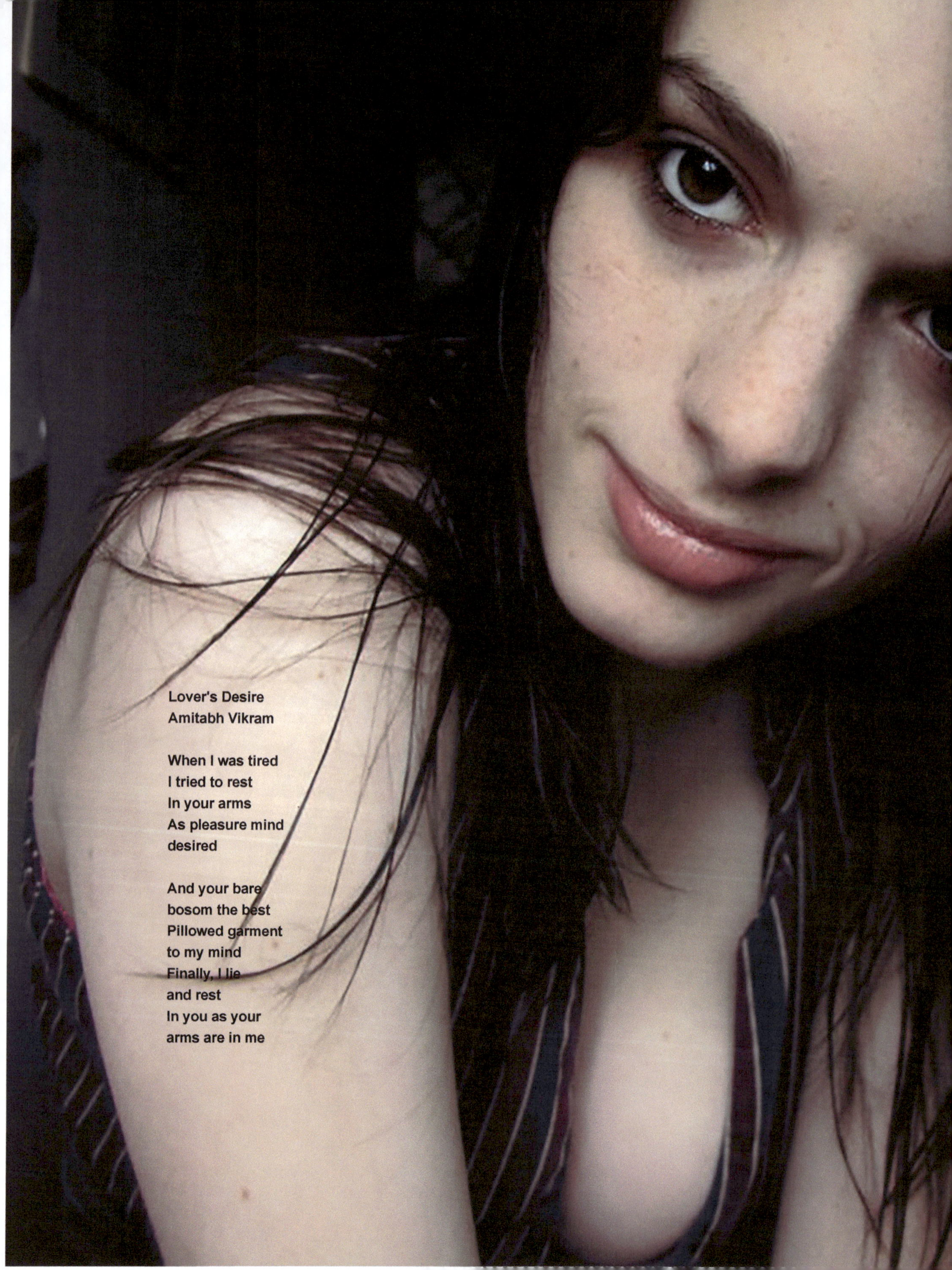

Lover's Desire
Amitabh Vikram

When I was tired
I tried to rest
In your arms
As pleasure mind
desired

And your bare
bosom the best
Pillowed garment
to my mind
Finally, I lie
and rest
In you as your
arms are in me

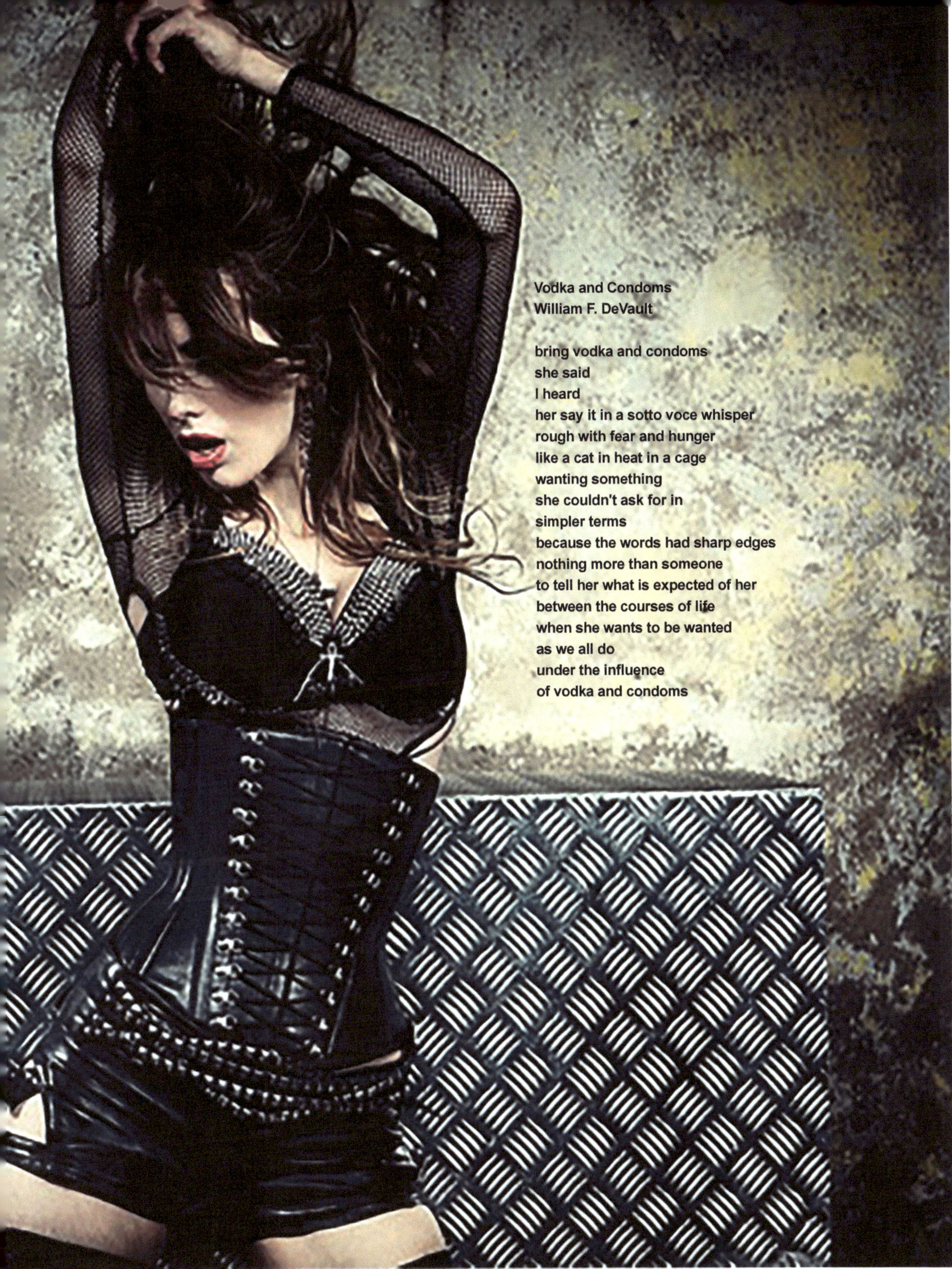

Vodka and Condoms
William F. DeVault

bring vodka and condoms
she said
I heard
her say it in a sotto voce whisper
rough with fear and hunger
like a cat in heat in a cage
wanting something
she couldn't ask for in
simpler terms
because the words had sharp edges
nothing more than someone
to tell her what is expected of her
between the courses of life
when she wants to be wanted
as we all do
under the influence
of vodka and condoms

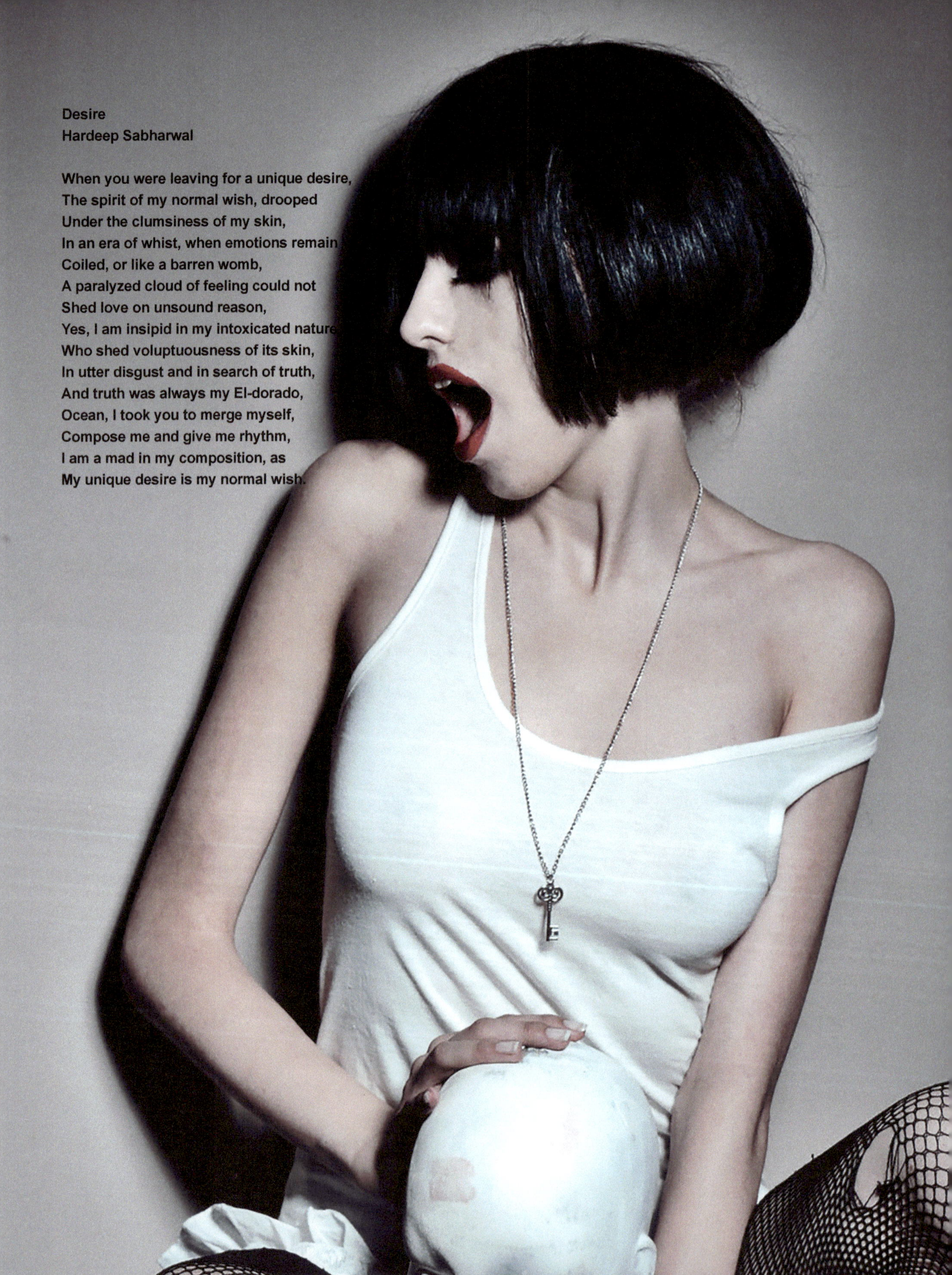

Desire
Hardeep Sabharwal

When you were leaving for a unique desire,
The spirit of my normal wish, drooped
Under the clumsiness of my skin,
In an era of whist, when emotions remain
Coiled, or like a barren womb,
A paralyzed cloud of feeling could not
Shed love on unsound reason,
Yes, I am insipid in my intoxicated nature
Who shed voluptuousness of its skin,
In utter disgust and in search of truth,
And truth was always my El-dorado,
Ocean, I took you to merge myself,
Compose me and give me rhythm,
I am a mad in my composition, as
My unique desire is my normal wish.

Last Poem for H.
Nate Maxson

In this brief, cool and dry place: this flash of an hour
Like a breath underground
We pass beneath a structure,
In my dreamlands: where my reflection on the water smirks knowingly
An inkblot in a field of stones worn down to a suggestion of statues
A suggestion of a wall or a cloud across the sun
Between twin shimmering Indian summers
I think of all the stories I've heard about people
Rushing into burning buildings
To save a child or a dog
And that I've never met someone who actually did it
Where have all the burning buildings gone?
I think of a fisherman's net that I once saw, hung on a wall in a museum
It was made of fine red string, what it must have looked like serrating the water…
All of this: a hindsight before I turn to salt
Flakes away like rust and dust and fireflies
Down to a low resolution memory
I am not Orpheus
And you are not Eurydice
Those are just ego dreams,
Like distant wildfires glowing
That wore out their invitation
Before evaporating
We passed by in midday shadow
Each only looking back
After the moment
Once

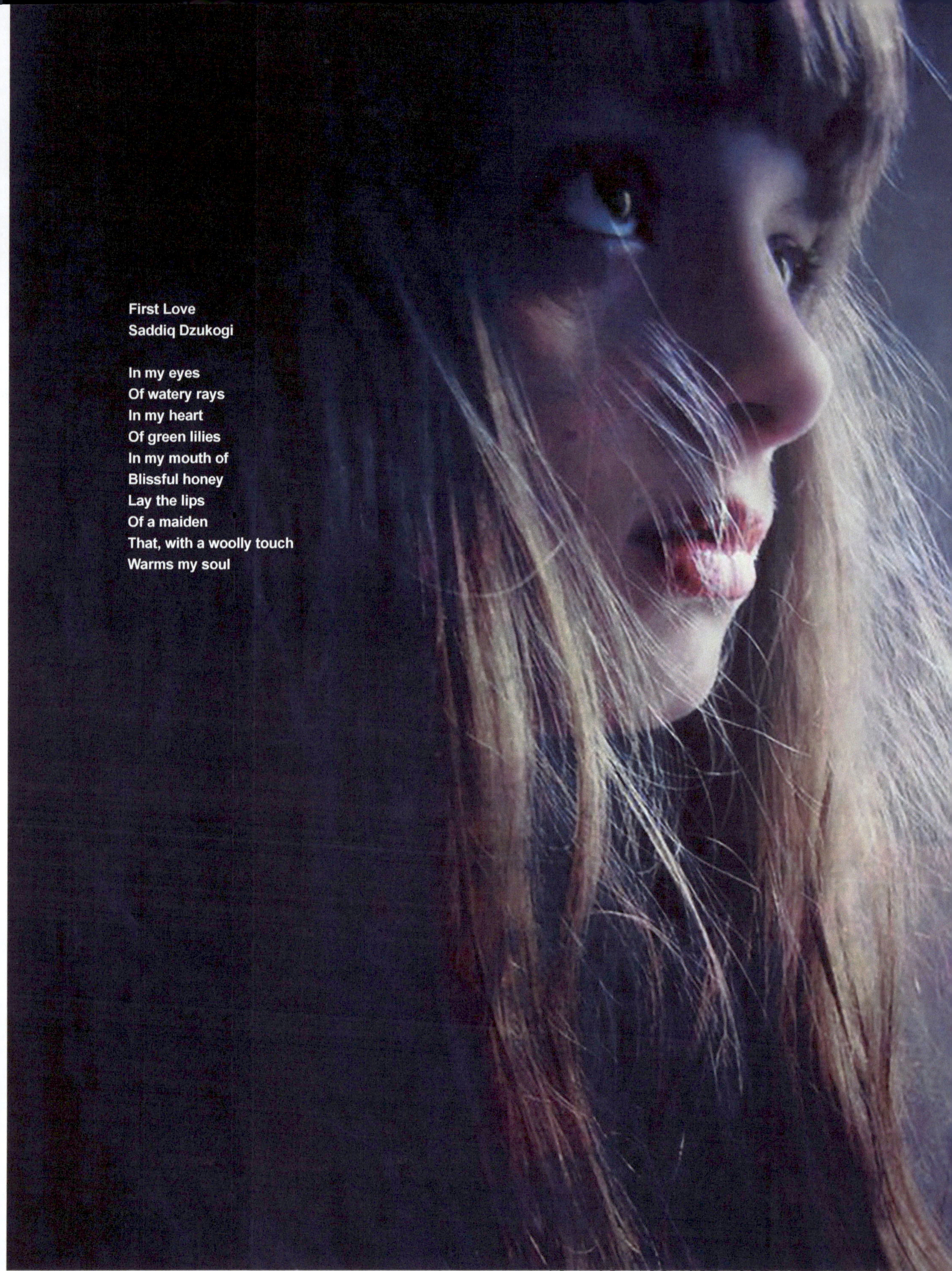

First Love
Saddiq Dzukogi

In my eyes
Of watery rays
In my heart
Of green lilies
In my mouth of
Blissful honey
Lay the lips
Of a maiden
That, with a woolly touch
Warms my soul

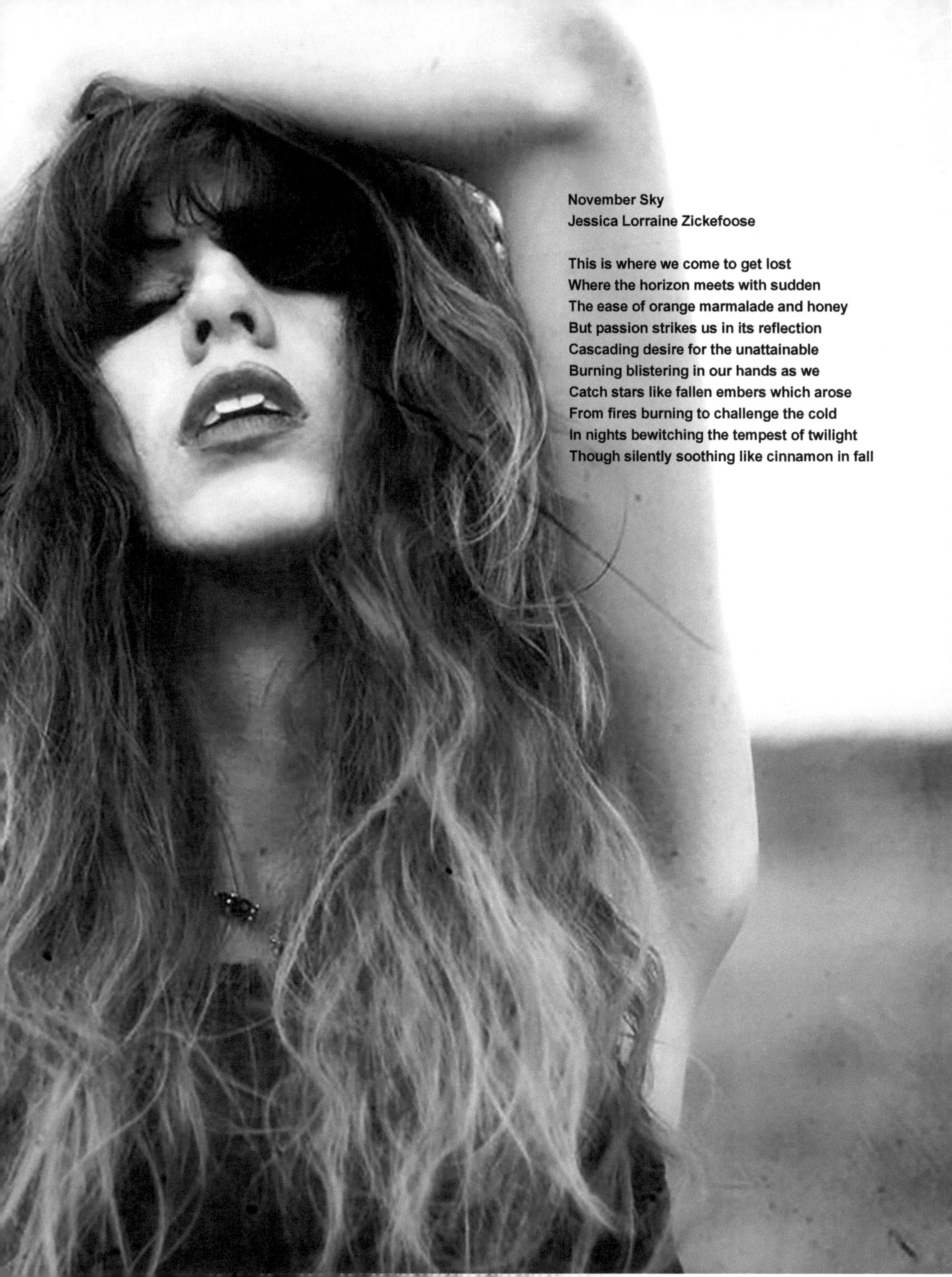

November Sky
Jessica Lorraine Zickefoose

This is where we come to get lost
Where the horizon meets with sudden
The ease of orange marmalade and honey
But passion strikes us in its reflection
Cascading desire for the unattainable
Burning blistering in our hands as we
Catch stars like fallen embers which arose
From fires burning to challenge the cold
In nights bewitching the tempest of twilight
Though silently soothing like cinnamon in fall

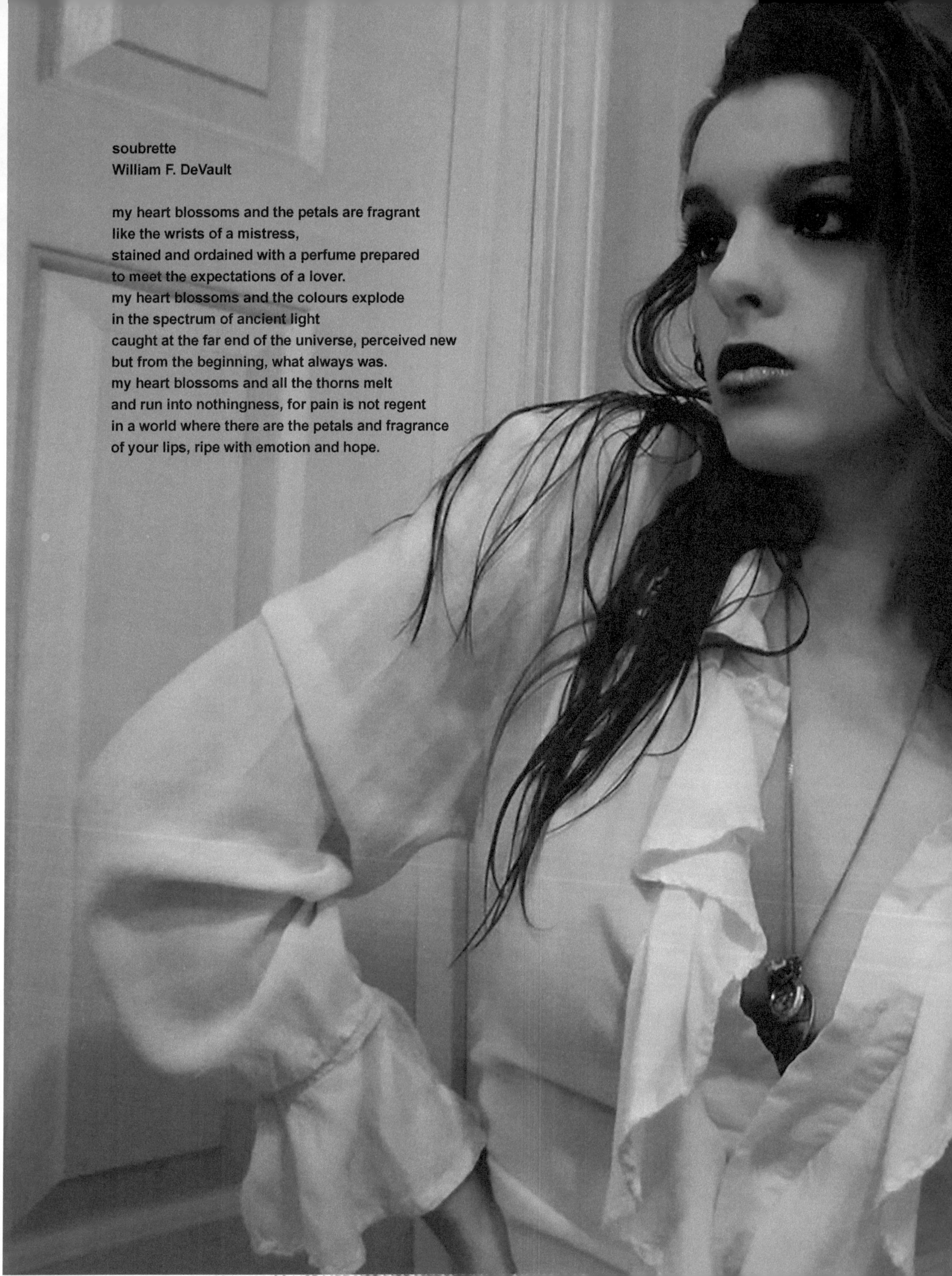

soubrette
William F. DeVault

my heart blossoms and the petals are fragrant
like the wrists of a mistress,
stained and ordained with a perfume prepared
to meet the expectations of a lover.
my heart blossoms and the colours explode
in the spectrum of ancient light
caught at the far end of the universe, perceived new
but from the beginning, what always was.
my heart blossoms and all the thorns melt
and run into nothingness, for pain is not regent
in a world where there are the petals and fragrance
of your lips, ripe with emotion and hope.

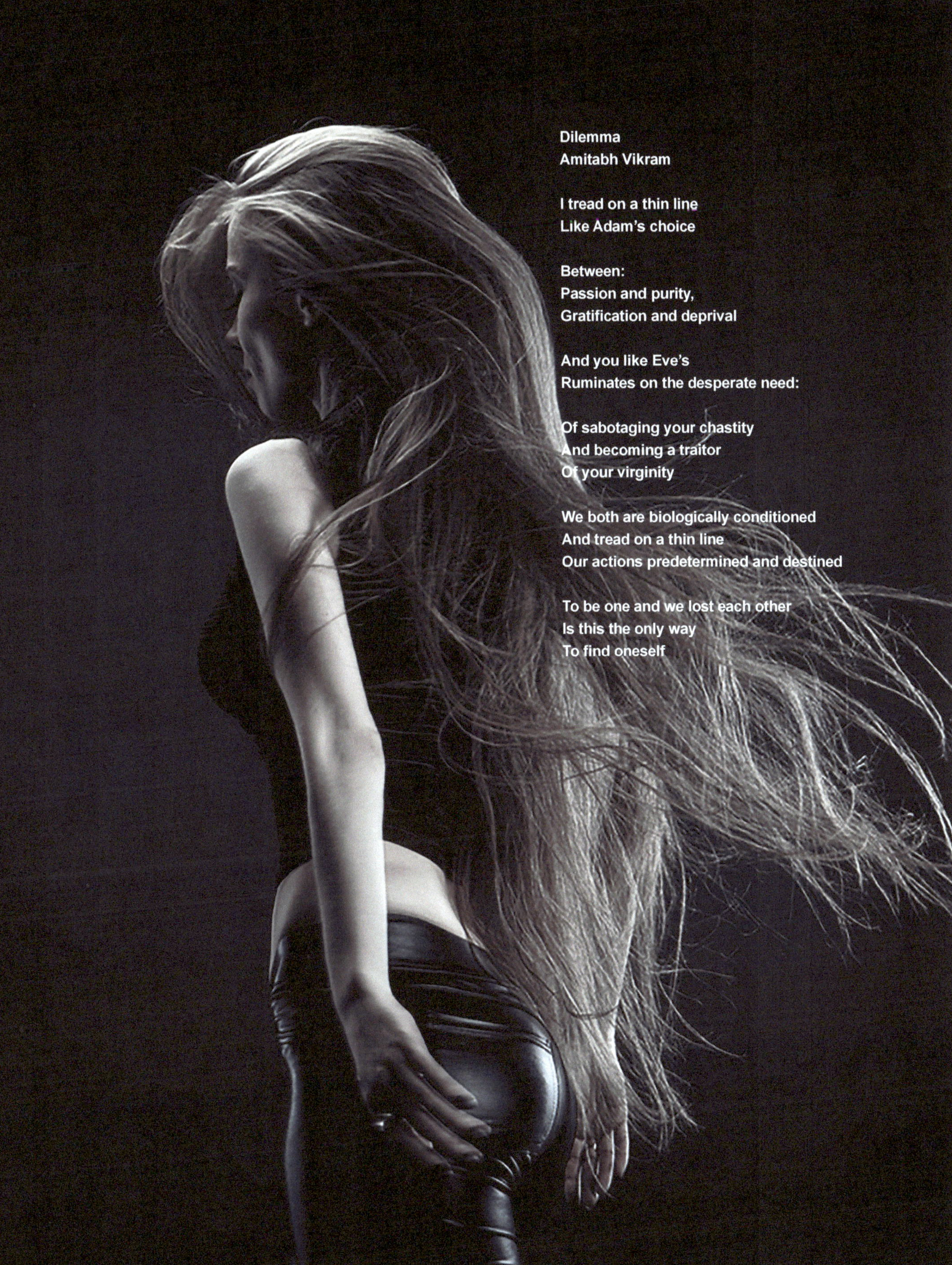

Dilemma
Amitabh Vikram

I tread on a thin line
Like Adam's choice

Between:
Passion and purity,
Gratification and deprival

And you like Eve's
Ruminates on the desperate need:

Of sabotaging your chastity
And becoming a traitor
Of your virginity

We both are biologically conditioned
And tread on a thin line
Our actions predetermined and destined

To be one and we lost each other
Is this the only way
To find oneself

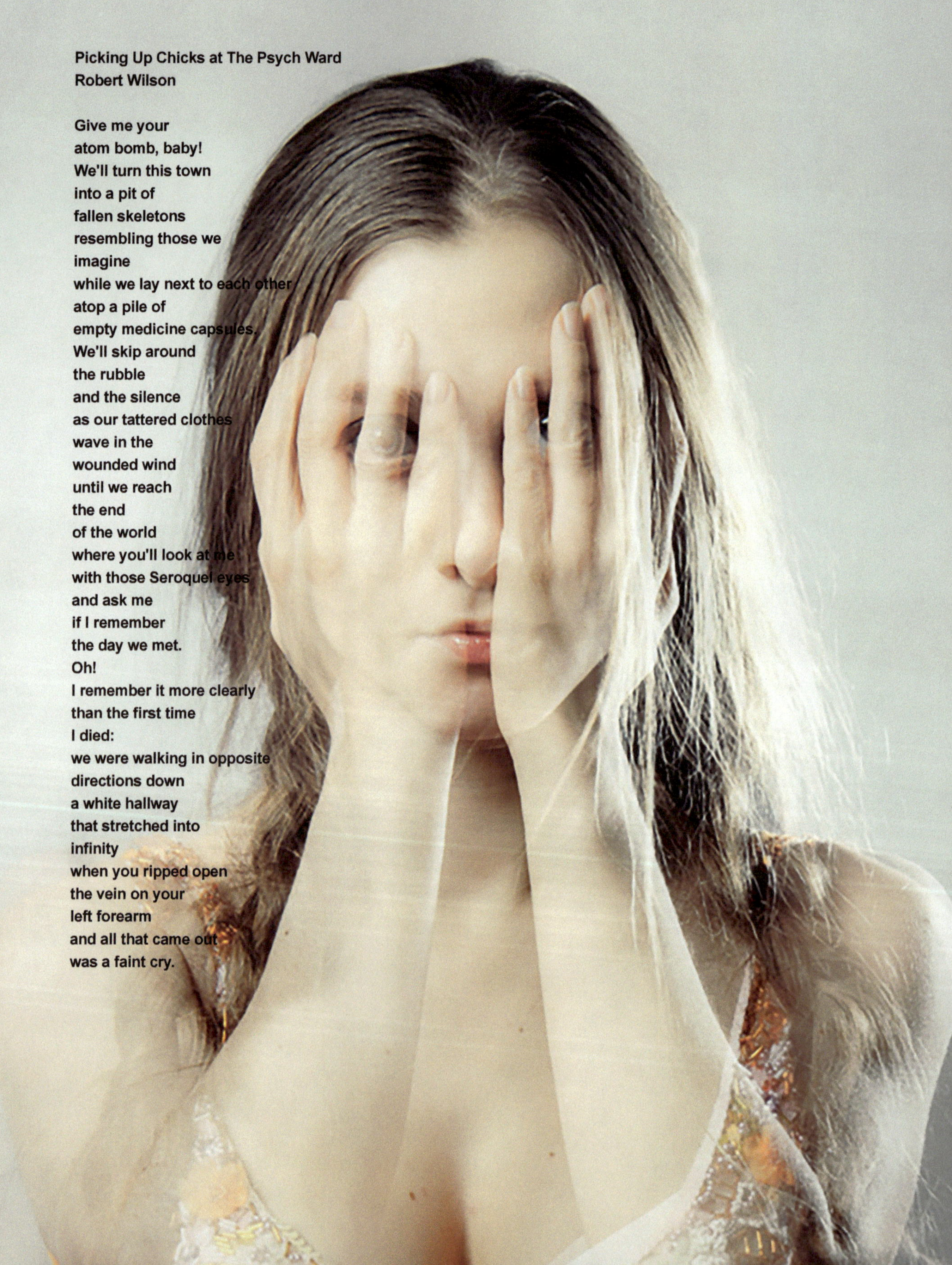

Picking Up Chicks at The Psych Ward
Robert Wilson

Give me your
atom bomb, baby!
We'll turn this town
into a pit of
fallen skeletons
resembling those we
imagine
while we lay next to each other
atop a pile of
empty medicine capsules.
We'll skip around
the rubble
and the silence
as our tattered clothes
wave in the
wounded wind
until we reach
the end
of the world
where you'll look at me
with those Seroquel eyes
and ask me
if I remember
the day we met.
Oh!
I remember it more clearly
than the first time
I died:
we were walking in opposite
directions down
a white hallway
that stretched into
infinity
when you ripped open
the vein on your
left forearm
and all that came out
was a faint cry.

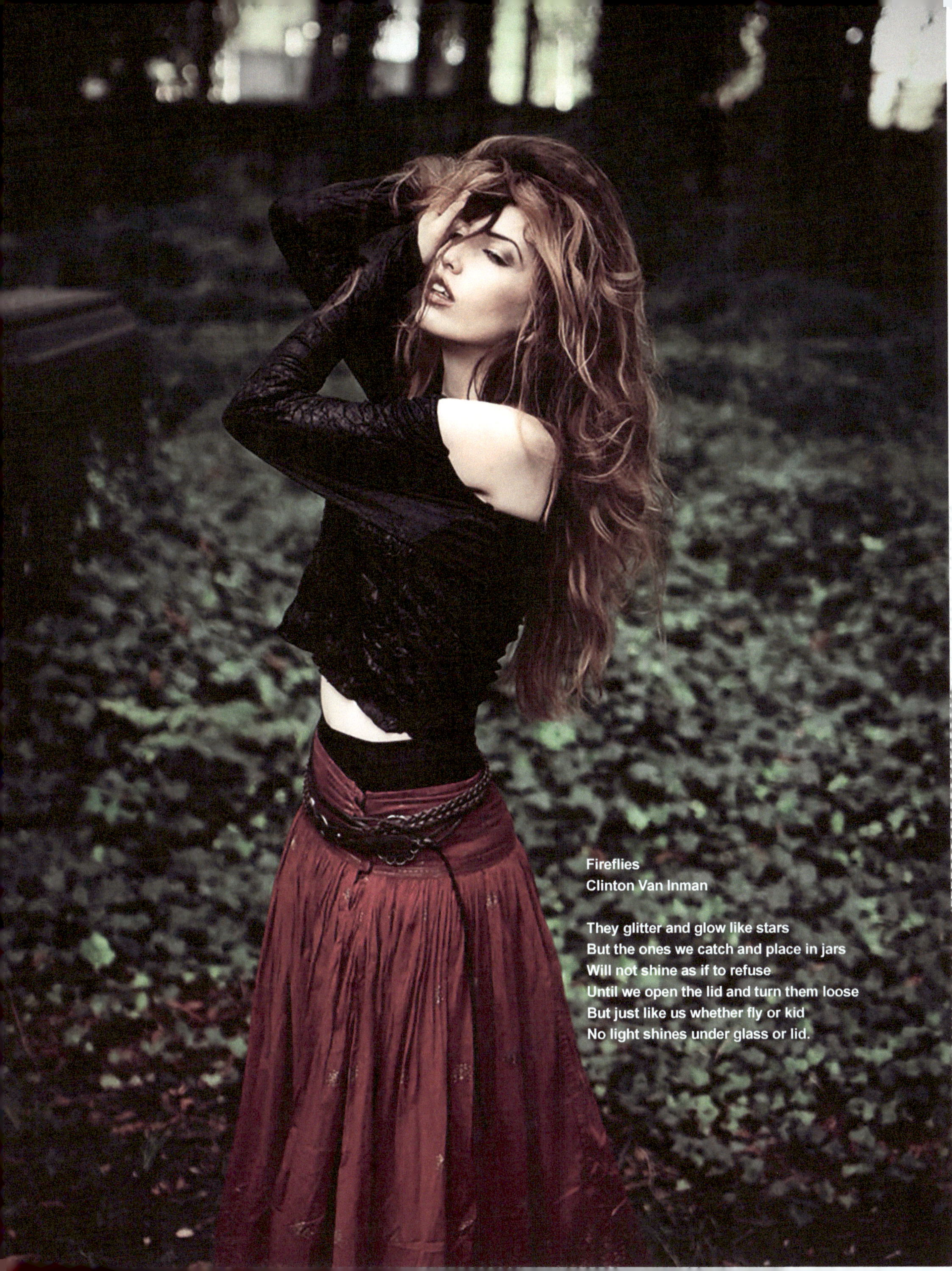

Fireflies
Clinton Van Inman

They glitter and glow like stars
But the ones we catch and place in jars
Will not shine as if to refuse
Until we open the lid and turn them loose
But just like us whether fly or kid
No light shines under glass or lid.

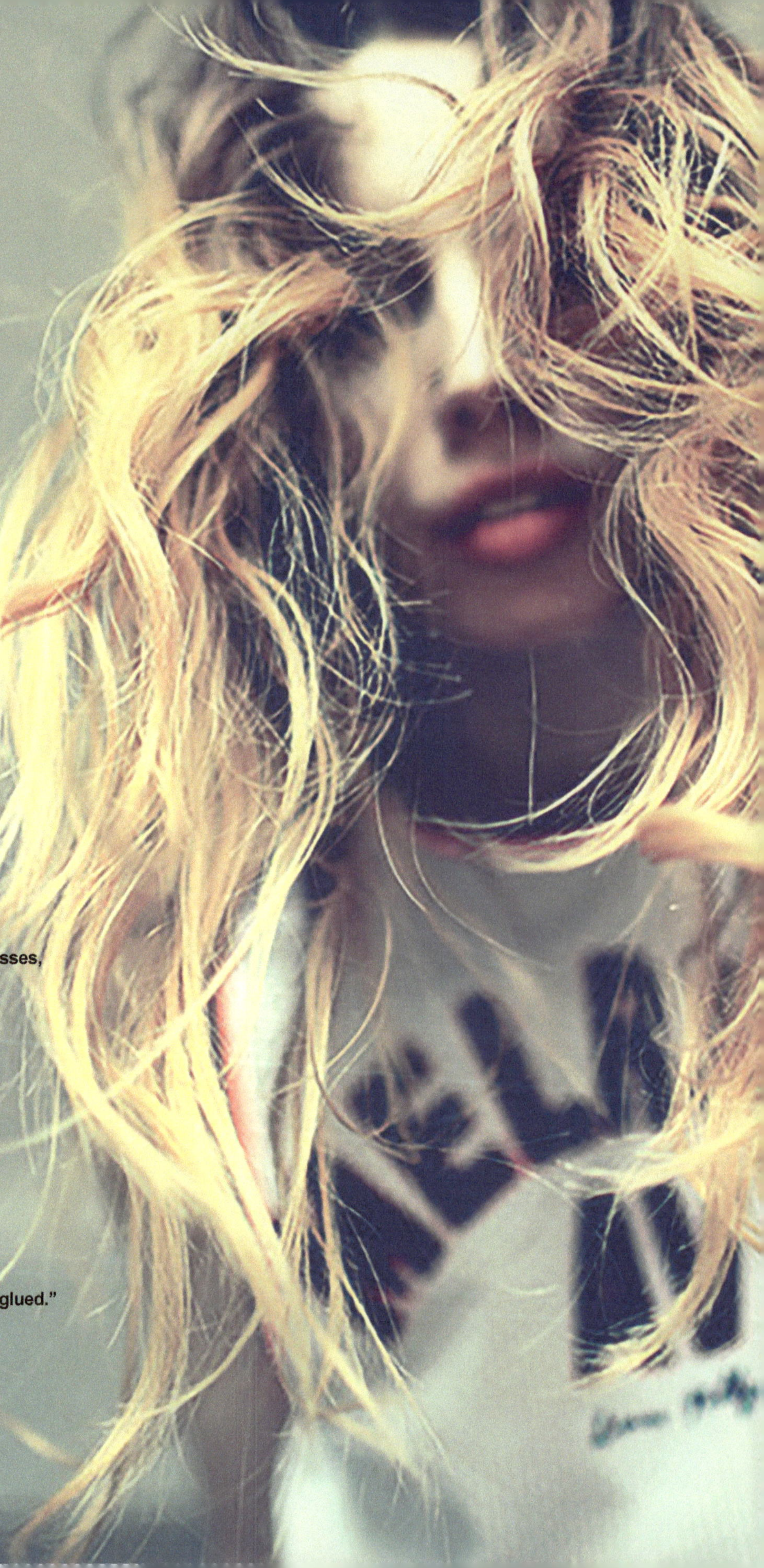

I'm Sorry We Were Ever Young
Robert Wilson

I fell in love with you
on the day Scott Weiland died.
We watched the darkness laugh,
held hands as the gears
collapsed around us,
danced in the Sheetz parking lot
with shadows splattered
in leprous sex.
Every time you pushed me away
I loved you more.
You would always pull me back
with a wink
and a kiss,
telling me
friendship is divinity
and love is God.
You strapped yourself to my back,
whispering
"We got this."
Meanwhile, I
tossed away the knives
to prevent a suicide.
Mine or yours,
I don't know
but I'm still trying to figure out
if it worked,
if we're both dead
outside your old apartment
with cuts
spelling out each other's mental illnesses,
performing BDSM
on each other's graves.
I wish I could beat this dead horse
to a life it never lived
but I know
there is apathy
where lust once dwelled
on your tongue
and nothing but anxiety
on mine.
I just want you to know
I still think of you
when I hear Stone Temple Pilots' "Unglued."
I rip myself apart
then put it all back together
without you.

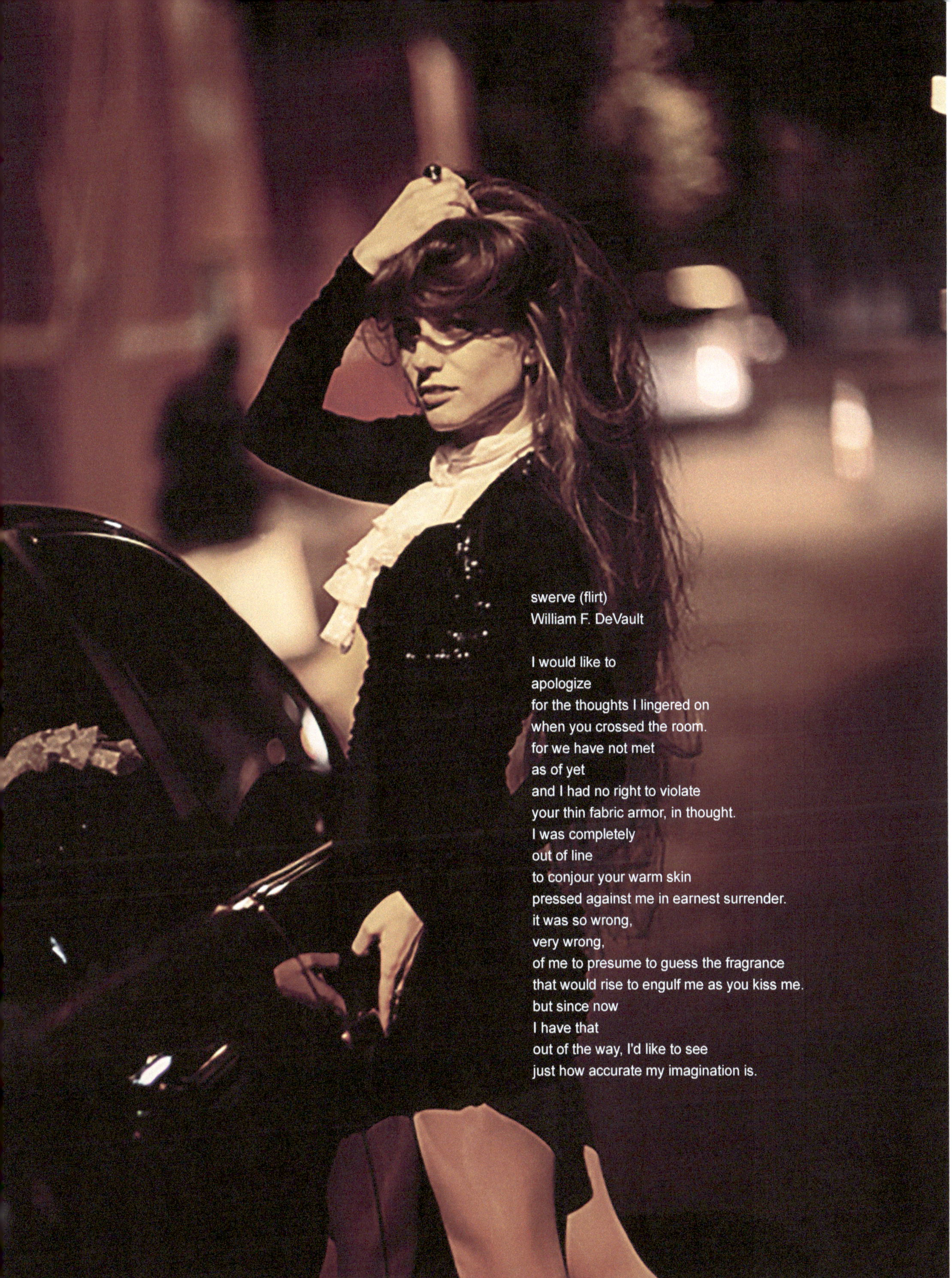

swerve (flirt)
William F. DeVault

I would like to
apologize
for the thoughts I lingered on
when you crossed the room.
for we have not met
as of yet
and I had no right to violate
your thin fabric armor, in thought.
I was completely
out of line
to conjour your warm skin
pressed against me in earnest surrender.
it was so wrong,
very wrong,
of me to presume to guess the fragrance
that would rise to engulf me as you kiss me.
but since now
I have that
out of the way, I'd like to see
just how accurate my imagination is.

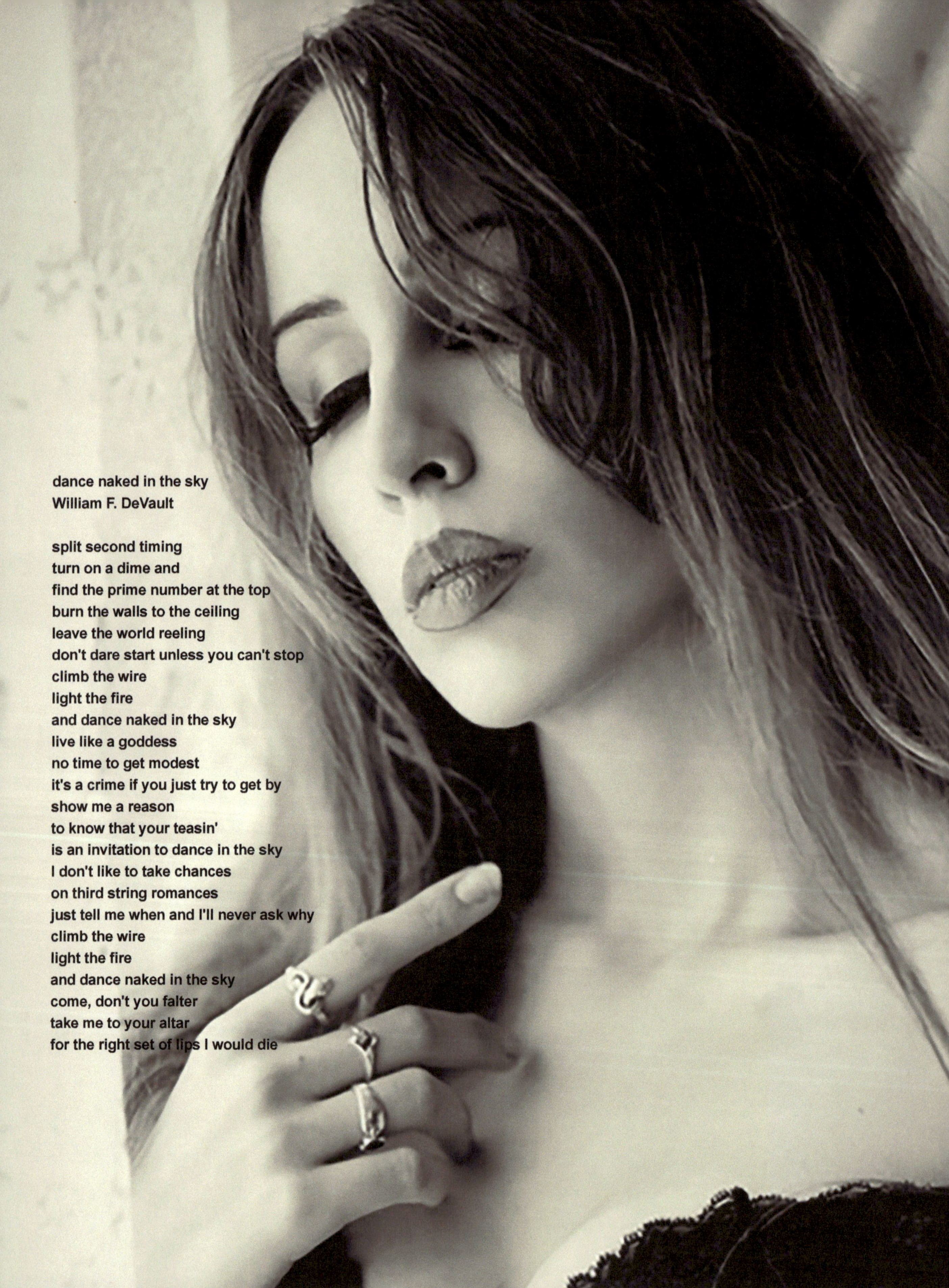

dance naked in the sky
William F. DeVault

split second timing
turn on a dime and
find the prime number at the top
burn the walls to the ceiling
leave the world reeling
don't dare start unless you can't stop
climb the wire
light the fire
and dance naked in the sky
live like a goddess
no time to get modest
it's a crime if you just try to get by
show me a reason
to know that your teasin'
is an invitation to dance in the sky
I don't like to take chances
on third string romances
just tell me when and I'll never ask why
climb the wire
light the fire
and dance naked in the sky
come, don't you falter
take me to your altar
for the right set of lips I would die

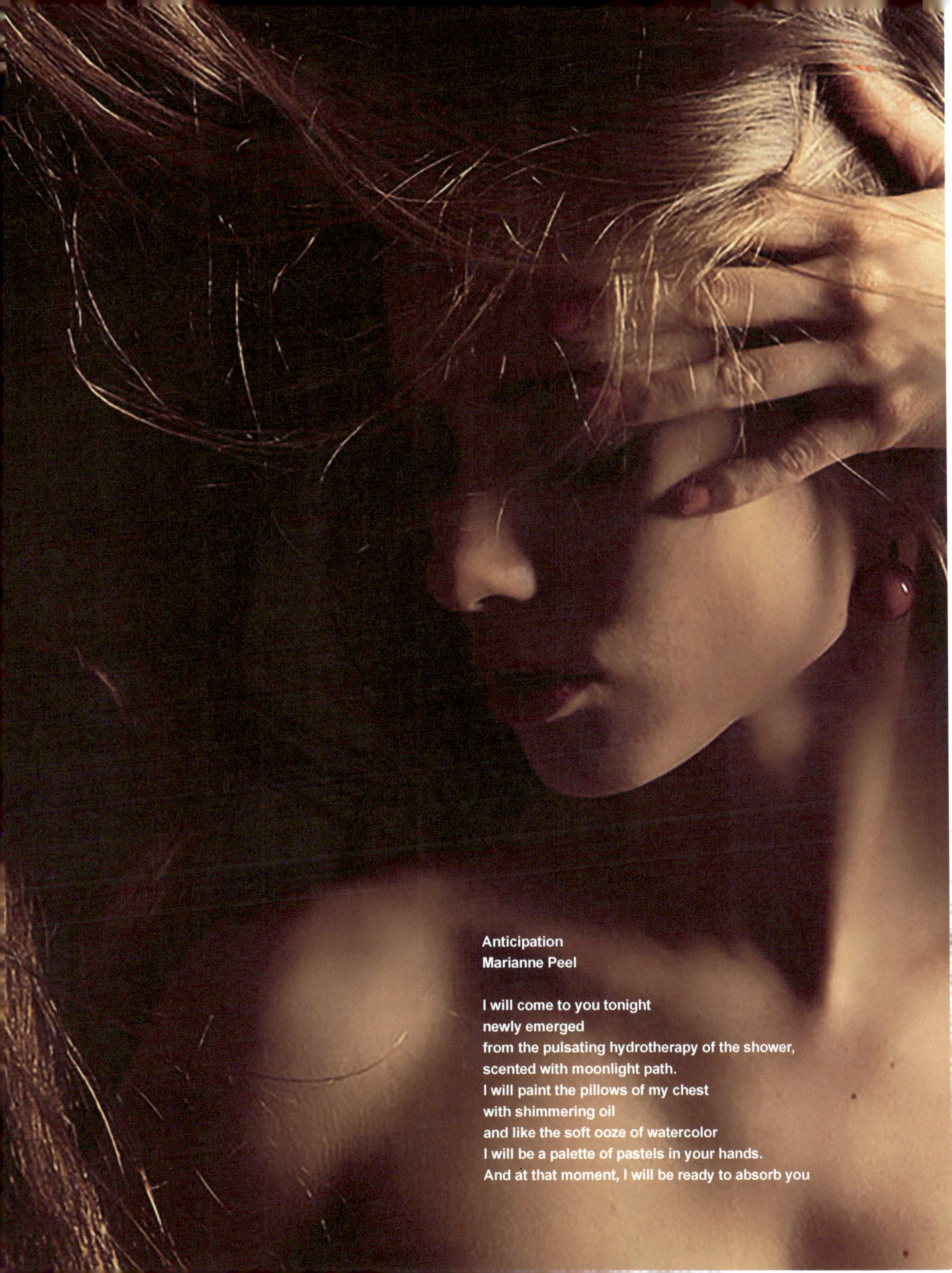

Anticipation
Marianne Peel

I will come to you tonight
newly emerged
from the pulsating hydrotherapy of the shower,
scented with moonlight path.
I will paint the pillows of my chest
with shimmering oil
and like the soft ooze of watercolor
I will be a palette of pastels in your hands.
And at that moment, I will be ready to absorb you

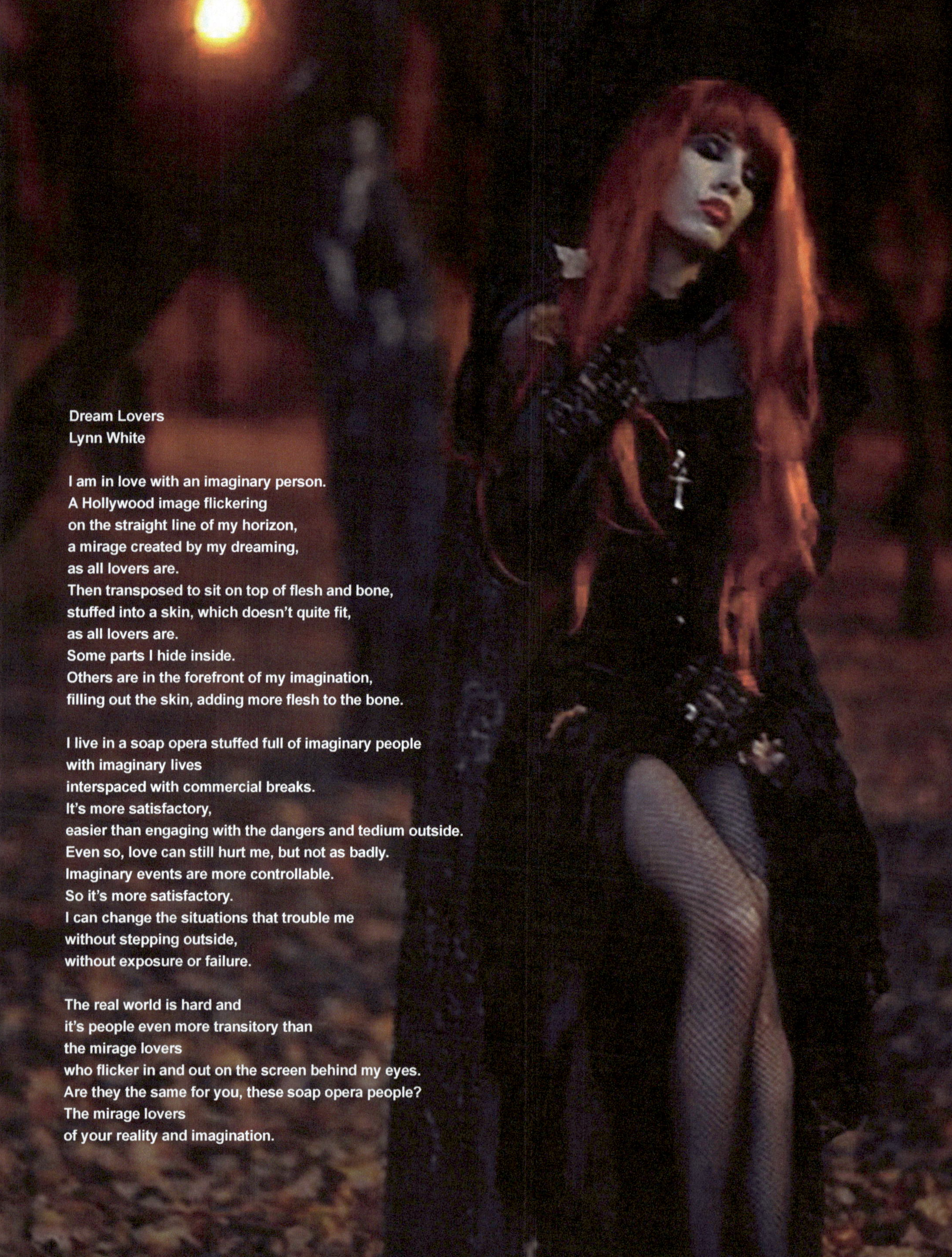

Dream Lovers
Lynn White

I am in love with an imaginary person.
A Hollywood image flickering
on the straight line of my horizon,
a mirage created by my dreaming,
as all lovers are.
Then transposed to sit on top of flesh and bone,
stuffed into a skin, which doesn't quite fit,
as all lovers are.
Some parts I hide inside.
Others are in the forefront of my imagination,
filling out the skin, adding more flesh to the bone.

I live in a soap opera stuffed full of imaginary people
with imaginary lives
interspaced with commercial breaks.
It's more satisfactory,
easier than engaging with the dangers and tedium outside.
Even so, love can still hurt me, but not as badly.
Imaginary events are more controllable.
So it's more satisfactory.
I can change the situations that trouble me
without stepping outside,
without exposure or failure.

The real world is hard and
it's people even more transitory than
the mirage lovers
who flicker in and out on the screen behind my eyes.
Are they the same for you, these soap opera people?
The mirage lovers
of your reality and imagination.

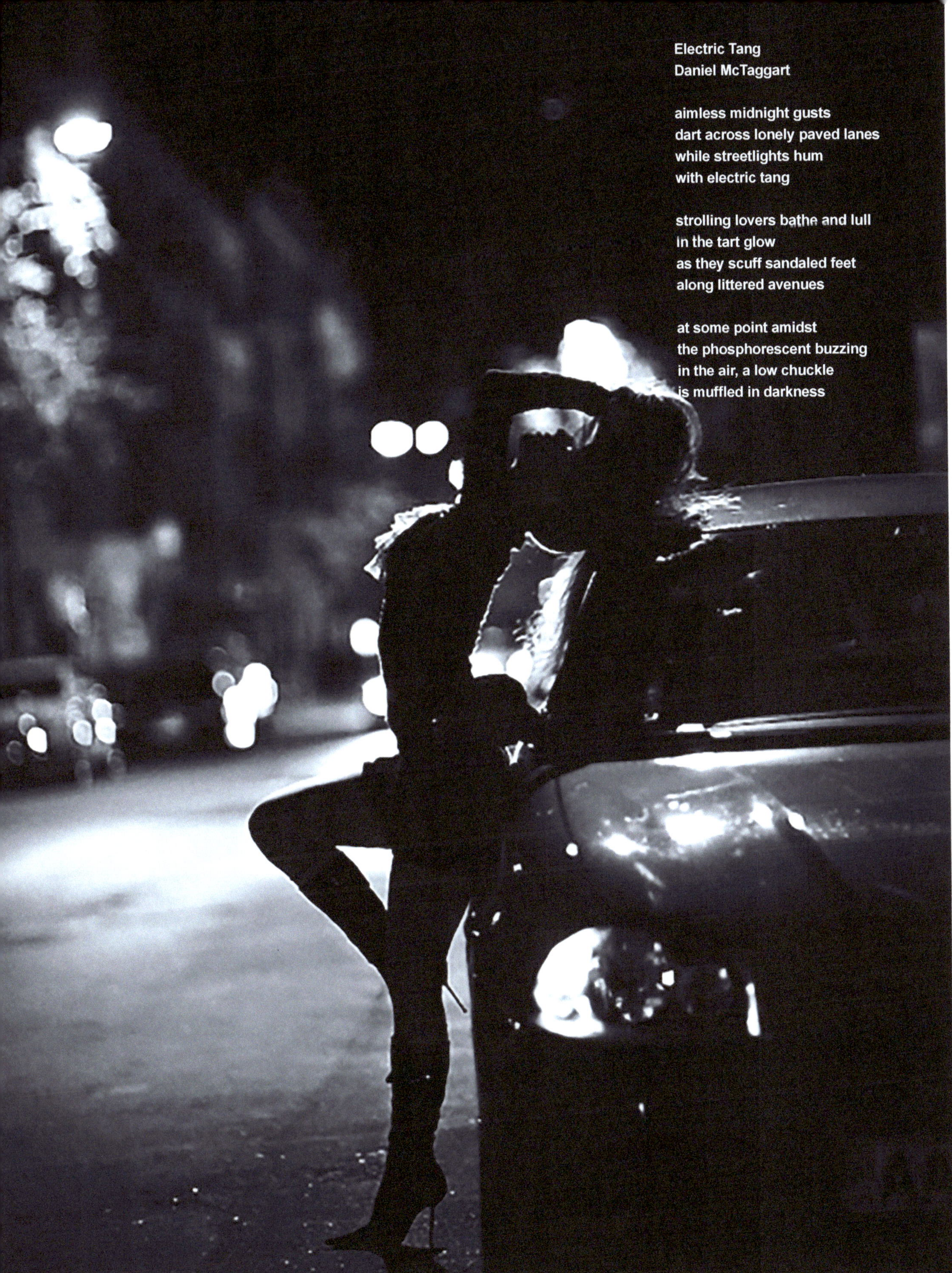

Electric Tang
Daniel McTaggart

aimless midnight gusts
dart across lonely paved lanes
while streetlights hum
with electric tang

strolling lovers bathe and lull
in the tart glow
as they scuff sandaled feet
along littered avenues

at some point amidst
the phosphorescent buzzing
in the air, a low chuckle
is muffled in darkness

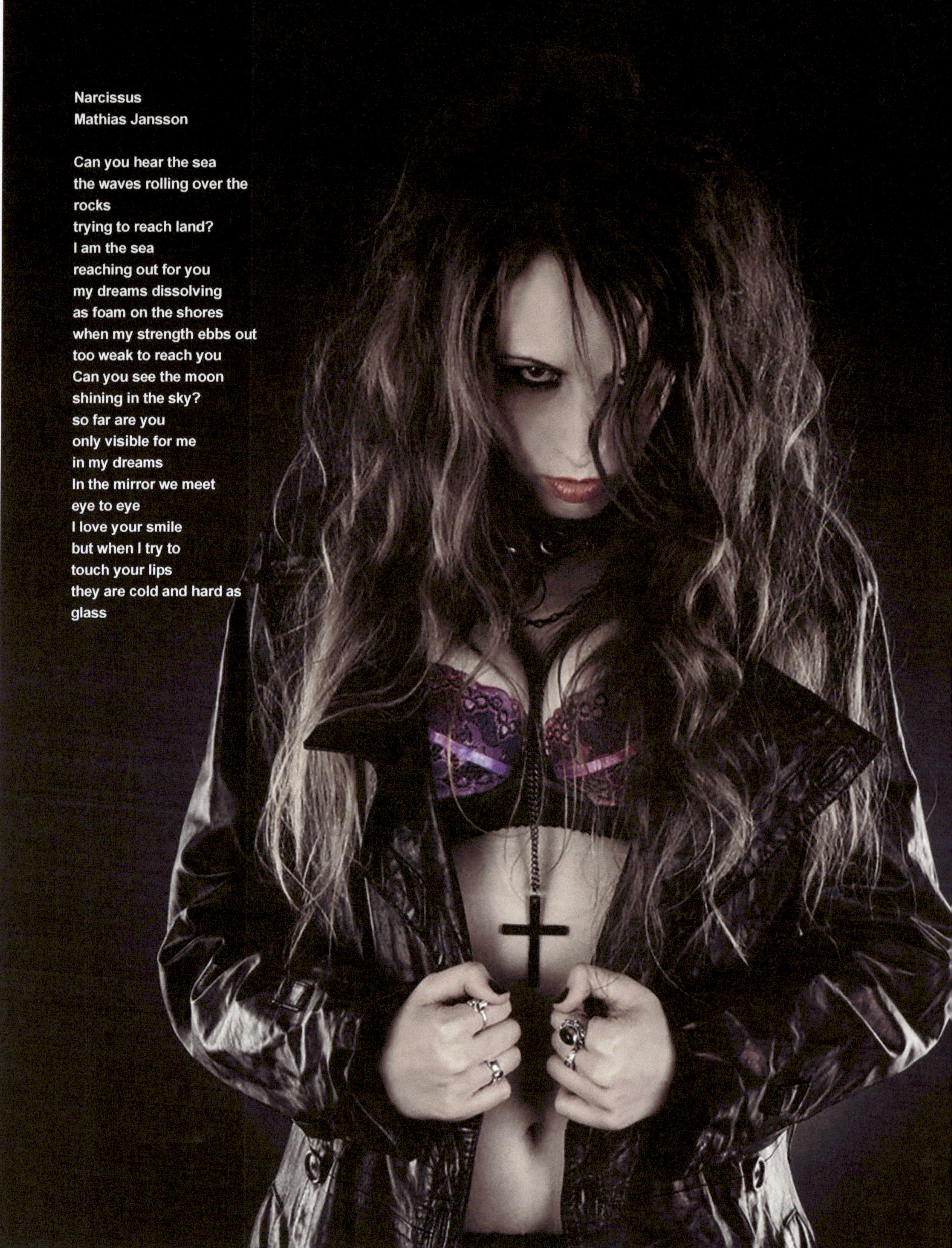

Narcissus
Mathias Jansson

Can you hear the sea
the waves rolling over the
rocks
trying to reach land?
I am the sea
reaching out for you
my dreams dissolving
as foam on the shores
when my strength ebbs out
too weak to reach you
Can you see the moon
shining in the sky?
so far are you
only visible for me
in my dreams
In the mirror we meet
eye to eye
I love your smile
but when I try to
touch your lips
they are cold and hard as
glass

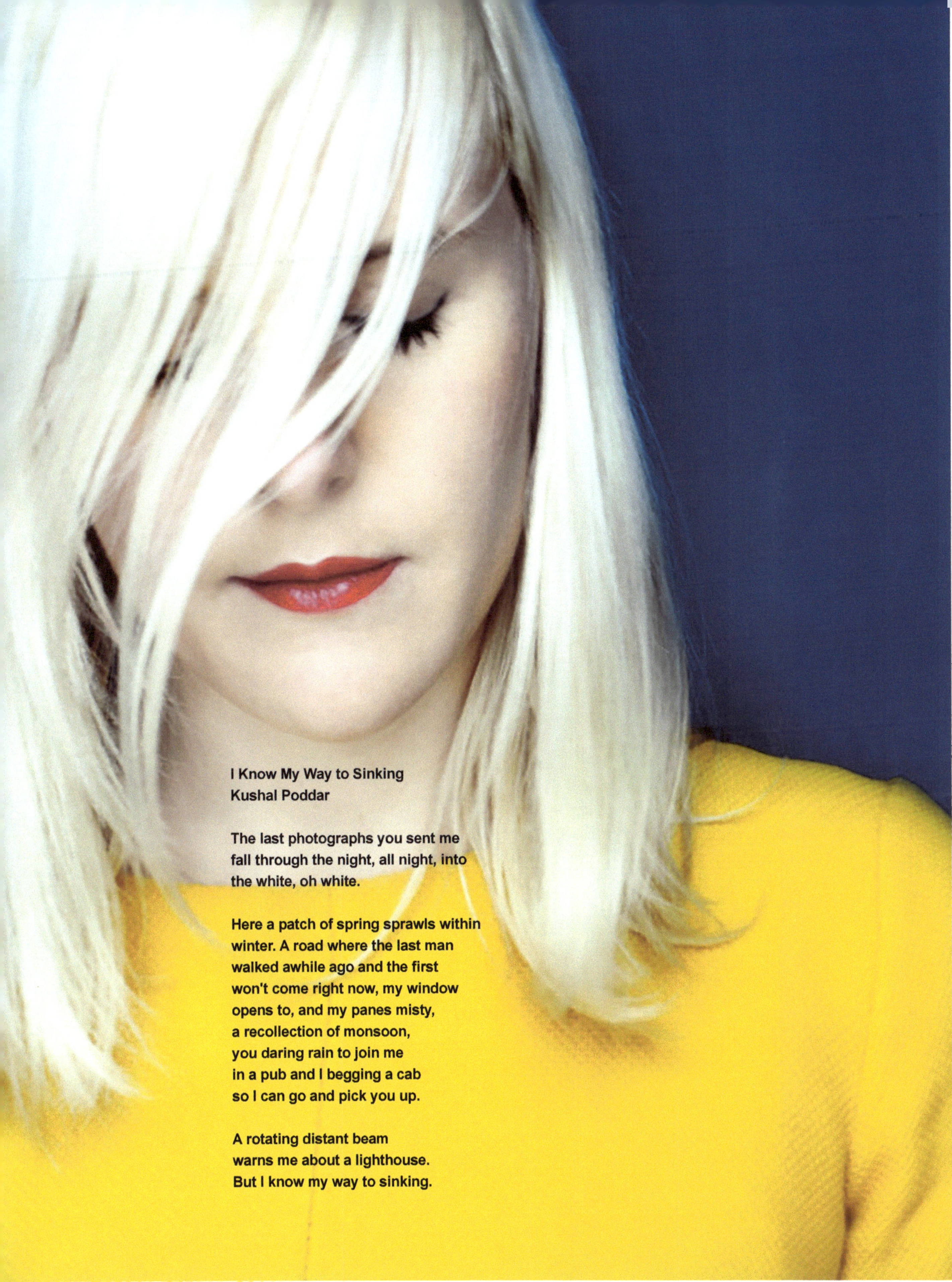

I Know My Way to Sinking
Kushal Poddar

The last photographs you sent me
fall through the night, all night, into
the white, oh white.

Here a patch of spring sprawls within
winter. A road where the last man
walked awhile ago and the first
won't come right now, my window
opens to, and my panes misty,
a recollection of monsoon,
you daring rain to join me
in a pub and I begging a cab
so I can go and pick you up.

A rotating distant beam
warns me about a lighthouse.
But I know my way to sinking.